KARAGHIOZIS

THREE MODERN GREEK SHADOW-PLAY COMEDIES

THE LITERARY WORK OF THEODORE STEPHANIDES

This is the third volume in the projected publication or republication by Colenso Books of all the original poetry, verse drama, stories and literary translations of Theodore Stephanides, including translations made in co-operation with George Katsimbalis and others. Only the titles with a date following in the list below have been published or will be published soon..

ORIGINAL POETRY, SHORT FICTION AND DRAMA BY STEPHANIDES

The Collected Poems of Theodore Stephanides
including the four published collections: *The Golden Face — Cities of the Mind — Worlds in a Crucible — Autumn Gleanings*, of which only the first (see below) and last are in print, and some additional poems

Το Χρυσό Προσωπείο / The Golden Face, Greek translation by Vera Konidari, with the original English *en face* (2019)

Stories Grim and Otherwise

The Complete Verse Dramas of Theodore Stephanides
(*Arodaphnousa — The Bridge of Arta — Labyrinth — All power corrupts*)

TRANSLATIONS BY STEPHANIDES ALONE

Sweet-voiced Sappho (2015)

Five Hundred Epigrams from the Greek Anthology (expected 2021)

Erotocritos by VITZENTZOS KORNAROS

Life, Love and Death in Modern Greek folk poetry

TRANSLATIONS BY STEPHANIDES AND KATSIMBALIS

Modern Greek Poetry: An Anthology (expected 2021)

Life Immutable, The King's Flute, The Twelve Words of the Gypsy, and Other Poems by KOSTIS PALAMAS

OTHER WORKS OF GREEK LITERATURE FROM COLENSO BOOKS

Three Plays by IAKOVOS KAMBANELLIS (*The Courtyard of Wonders —The Four Legs of the Table — Ibsenland*), translated by Marjorie Chambers (2015)

The Life and Death of Hangman Thomas (2016) — *Corfiot Tales* (2017)
What price honour? – The Convict: two novellas (2020)
all by KONSTANTINOS THEOTOKIS and translated by J. M. Q. Davies

Yannis Ritsos among his contemporaries: twentieth-century Greek poetry (2018)
translated by Marjorie Chambers

Karaghiozis

THREE MODERN GREEK
SHADOW-PLAY COMEDIES

Doctor Karaghiozis

Karaghiozis and the Enchanted Tree

*Karaghiozis, Alexander the Great,
and the Dreadful Dragon*

TRANSLATED BY

Theodore Stephanides

EDITED BY

Anthony Hirst and Patrick Sammon

COLENSO BOOKS
2020

First published December 2020 by Colenso Books

Colenso Books
68 Palatine Road, London N16 8ST, UK
colensobooks@gmail.com

ISBN 978-0-9928632-6-5

Foreword, Translations and some Notes
Copyright © 2020 the Estate of Theodore Stephanides

Introduction and other Notes
Copyright © 2020 Colenso Books

Two of the three shadow-plays comedies in this volume were previously published in *The Greek Gazette* (London):
Doctor Karaghiozis, together with the Foreword
in Vol. 13, No. 137 (January 1979);
Karaghiozis and the Enchanted Tree
in Vol. 13, No. 148 (December 1979).

Karahiozis, Alexander the Great, and the Dreadful Dragon
is published here for the first time.

Enquiries about performance rights should be directed
in the first instance to Colenso Books.

The texts of the three shadow-plays area based on typescripts
in the Theodore Stephanides Archive now in the British Library
(see Sources, pages xi–xiii).

The illustrations on the front and back covers, on the title pages
of the individual shadow-play texts and on certain other pages
are scans of articulated cardboard puppets,
also in the Theodore Stephanides Archive.

CONTENTS

Introduction by Anthony Hirst	vii
Sources	xi
Guide to the pronunciation of names and titles	xiv
Foreword: A short study of the Greek popular shadow-show by Theodore Stephanides	1
Doctor Karaghiozis	7
Persons	8
Act One	9
Act Two	17
Act Three	28
Karaghiozis and the Enchanted Tree	43
Persons	44
Act One	45
Act Two	49
Act Three	53
Karaghiozis, Alexander the Great, and the Dreadful Dragon	61
Persons	62
Act One	63
Act Two	68
Act Three	75
Act Four	79
Notes	86

INTRODUCTION

This is the third volume in the projected Complete Works (original writings and translations) of Theodore Stephanides, but only the second one based on archival materials. Since Stephanides' Sappho translations were published as *Sweet-voiced Sappho*, my reliance on copies of typescripts lodged by Stephanides himself in the British Library and other libraries has been much reduced by the rediscovery of Stephanides' literary papers (referred to below as the Stephanides Archive) in the cellar of the London house where he spent the last decade of his life. This material is now in the British Library.

In the Archive I found typescripts of items I had feared might no longer exist, such as the original verse dramas *Arodaphnousa* and *The Bridge of Arta*, and the translation of *Five hundred epigrams from the Greek Anthology* and these three Karaghiozis playscripts; and also other items of which I had no previous knowledge, including another original verse drama *All power corrupts*, a substantial collection of original short stories, many unpublished original poems, and translations of haiku and tanka by Dimitris Andoniou and of poems by Lilika Papanikolaou.

Two of the three translations of shadow-play comedies in this volume have been published before, over forty years ago, in *The Greek Gazette* (London), which described itself as a "Monthly Journal for promoting Anglo-Hellenic Understanding". It was in the large format of newspapers of those days, but printed on much better quality paper than newsprint. *Doctor Karaghiozis* appeared in Vol. 13, No. 137 (January 1979) and *Karaghiozis and the Enchanted Tree* in Vol. 13, No. 148 (December 1979). The third translation, *Karaghiozis, Alexander the Great, and the Dreadful Dragon*, is published here for the first time.

There are multiple typescript or manuscript versions of all three shadow-play translations in the Stephanides Archive. For details see "Sources" following this Introduction.

INTRODUCTION

Beyond correcting typing errors, making some changes to punctuation in the interest of clarity, and modifying the relation between character names preceding speeches, stage directions and the speeches themselves to conform to Colenso Books house style, I have made almost no editorial changes to the texts of the plays, other than changing the spelling of some of the characters' names to approximate more closely to Greek pronunciation; this last applies also to personal and place names in Stephanides' Foreword.

The Foreword was written to accompany *Doctor Karaghiozis* and required some adaptation to serve as the Foreword to this collection of three plays. In the typescripts each of the other two plays has its own brief Foreword, referring readers to the Foreword to *Doctor Karaghiozis* for further information, and adding some details about translation strategy. The last two paragraphs of the present Foreword combine what was the fourth paragraph of the Foreword to *Doctor Karaghiozis* with the additional material from the Forewords to the other two plays, with some phrases and a final sentence added by myself.

In stage directions, Stephanides sometimes uses the English forms *exits* (singular) and *exit* (plural) and sometimes the Latin forms *exit* (singular) and *exeunt* (plural). The Latin forms predominate, and where the English forms occur I have replaced them by the Latin forms. It looks as though Stephanides' model for this (as for other details, such as the heading "Persons" for the character lists) was the published versions of the verse plays of T. S. Eliot. I believe that Eliot's plays influenced Stephanides' own verse dramas, and particularly *The Labyrinth*, the only one set in the recent past.

The typescripts include a few footnotes. Patrick Sammon and I have collected these together, with additional notes supplied by ourselves, in a separate Notes section at the back of the book. Asterisks in the text indicate that information relating to the preceding word or phrase will be found among the Notes.

Both in the typescripts and the version published in *The Greek Gazette*, *Doctor Karaghiozis* is given the subtitle *A short study of the Greek popular shadow-show*. I have reassigned this subtitle to the Foreword where it more obviously belongs.

In the typescripts each of the plays has the subtitle *A Modern Greek shadow-play comedy*. Here this has been adapted to serve as the subtitle of the volume.

The images on the cover and on the title pages for each of the three play scripts are all from a series of cardboard Karaghiozis characters in the Stephanides Archive. The figures are articulated and held together with brass split pins (the heads of the pins are clearly visible in the images). The cardboard is relatively thin and the figures were not designed for serious performance, but were probably produced for children. They have been cut out by hand, apparently with scissors for the outside lines and a sharp blade for the interior holes. Many of them have the names of the characters written on the back in red felt-tip pen, but the handwriting is not that of Stephanides.

As Stephanides explains in the Foreword, he was not translating any particular puppeteer's script for these Karaghiozis shadow plays (and a great deal of improvisation was probably involved in any particular performance in any case). Instead, he has synthesized his own versions from recollections of multiple performances that he witnessed at various times and in various places in Greece in the period between the two World Wars, and in so doing he has adapted some of the humour to an English audience (references for example to the liner the *Queen Mary*, to beefsteak pie and fish and chips, and to sums of money in the old UK currency of pounds, shillings and pence). There are many puns, invented words and malapropisms which show Stephanides' inventiveness and skill in comic writing, which is also often evident in his own original poetry in English.

For many years Stephanides and Lawrence Durrell entertained the idea of collaborating on a book about Karaghiozis; and with this in mind, during 1954, Stephanides sent to Durrell his own "Notes on Karaghiozis" (far more extensive than his Foreword to this volume), and a series of translations he had made of then recent Greek publications on Karaghiozis, as well as his retyping of the greater part of a work on Karaghiozis in French published in 1921 (the book by Louis Rousel that he refers to in the Foreword). I had thought of including this material in the present volume, but realizing that, given the extent of it, the actual play texts would have been overwhelmed, I decided it would be better to reserve it for a later, separate publication of *Karaghiozis Studies*.

I would like to express my gratitude to Michelle McGaughey who retyped the three play scripts in a very tightly defined format for this book, so that very little further typesetting was required; to my co-editor, Patrick Sammon, who proofread the book at three different stages, and made many invaluable suggestions; and, above all, to Theodore Stephanides' two grandsons, Alexander and Pyrrhus Mercouris, for their permission, and indeed their encouragement, to continue with the publication of their grandfather's works, following the death in 2018 of their mother, Theodore's daughter, Alexia Stephanides-Mercouri.

A letter signed by Alexia some months before her death, authorising me to publish any and all of Theodore Stephanides' works has been lodged with the British Library, which now owns most of the surviving physical archival materials. Copies of some of his typescripts were deposited by Stephanides in various other libraries in the UK and USA, mostly in the 1970s.

Attempts to contact anyone who still represents the interests of *The Greek Gazette*, where two of the plays in this volume were first published, have so far proved unsuccessful. But I hope this may be remedied in the future. The British Library Catalogue suggests that *The Greek Gazette*, founded in 1967, ceased publication in 1997.

I hope that readers will get as much pleasure and laughter out of these comedies as I have done — this is certainly a book as much for children as for adults, and I look forward to giving copies to my younger grandchildren.

ANTHONY HIRST
LONDON, APRIL 2020

SOURCES

Reference numbers AT1–AT10 refer to a catalogue of the Stephanides Archive which I made immediately after the rediscovery of Stephanides' papers (see the Introduction), and about a year before their transfer to the British Library. Inn my catalogue each of the physically discrete assemblages of items (large envelopes, folders, boxes) was given an alphabetic number in the ranges A–Z, AA–AZ, BA–BZ and CA–CC. Individual items within the assemblages were identified by the addition of an arabic numeral. In the case of AT1–AT10, one manuscript and nine typescripts of the individual shadow plays in this volume, the arabic numbers were assigned arbitrarily as the materials came to hand and before any consideration of their relative dating was undertaken. In the British Library's Archives and Manuscripts Catalogue all of the Karaghiozis materials listed below have the reference "Theodore Stephanides Archive Add MS 89407/1/25" (and "AT" is given as the "former identifier"). The cardboard figures used for the illustrations on the front cover and on the title pages of the individual shadow-play scripts in this volume have the same British Library reference but with 26 in place of 25 at the end.

DOCTOR KARAGHIOZIS

Typescripts AT9 and AT10

"DOCTOR KARAGHIOSIS / A MODERN GREEK / SHADOW-PLAY COMEDY". Identical and identically corrected top copy (AT9) and carbon copy (AT10). Bound typescripts, with green card cover, on quarto paper, 41 sheets. Identical printed title labels on the covers read "DOCTOR KARAGHIOSIS / A SHORT STUDY OF THE GREEK POPULAR SHADOW-SHOW". Both copies dated "1978" on the inside back cover. AT9 is used as the basis of the text presented in this volume.

KARAGHIOZIS AND THE ENCHANTED TREE

Typescript AT6

"KARAGHIOZIS AND THE ENCHANTED TREE / A Modern Greek Shadow-Play Comedy in Three Acts". Carbon copy bound typescript, with manuscript corrections, reused quarto paper, 14 sheets, with brown wrapping-paper cover. Typed label on cover reads "KARAGHIOZIS / & THE ENCHANTED TREE / A Modern Greek Shadow-Play". Undated.

Typescripts AT7 and AT8

"KARAGHIOZIS AND THE ENCHANTED TREE / A Modern Greek Shadow-Play Comedy in Three Acts". Identical top copy (AT7) and carbon copy (AT8). Bound typescripts with brown wrapping-paper covers, quarto paper, 17 numbered sheets and one blank sheet at the end. Dated on the title page October 1979. The manuscript corrections in AT6 are an integral part of the text, indicating that AT7/8 is a later draft. AT7 is used as the basis for the text presented in this volume.

KARAGHIOZIS, ALEXANDER THE GREAT, AND THE DREADFUL DRAGON

Manuscript AT1

"KARAGHIOSIS / ALEXANDER THE GREAT & THE DREADFUL DRAGON / A Modern Greek Shadow-play Comedy in Four Acts". Fair-copy manuscript, with some corrections, on lined foolscap paper, 22 sheets, with brown wrapping-paper cover. No title on cover. Dated July 1980 on second sheet. Evidently the first of four drafts (see *Typescript AT5* below).

Typescript AT5

"KARAGIOZIS, ALEXANDER THE GREAT, / AND THE DREADFUL DRAGON / A Modern Greek Shadow-Play Comedy in Four Acts" (in "KARAGIOZIS" H has been added after G by hand to correct to "KARAGHIOZIS"). Top-copy typescript on unlined quarto paper, 23 numbered sheets and one blank sheet at the end, with brown wrapping-paper cover. Typed title label on cover reads "K A R A G H I O Z I S / ALEXANDER THE GREAT / & THE DREADFUL DRAGON / A Modern Greek / Shadow-show Comedy". Page breaks do not coincide with those of AT4 (below) after sheet 7, and the text ends further down sheet 23. Dated July 1980 on the title sheet. Corrections in *Manuscript AT1* incorporated in the typing; further manuscript corrections. Evidently the second draft.

Typescript AT4

Title identical to that of AT5, except that the H of KARA-GHIOZIS is integral to the typing. Top-copy typescript on unlined quarto paper, 23 numbered sheets and one blank sheet at the end, with brown wrapping-paper cover. Typed label on the cover identical to that of AT5. Dated July 1980 on the title sheet. Some of the manuscript corrections in AT5 are an integral part of the typing, indicating that this is the third draft; further manuscript corrections.

Typescripts AT2 and AT3

"KARAGHIOZIS, ALEXANDER THE GREAT AND / THE DREADFUL DRAGON / A Modern Greek Shadow-Play Comedy in Four Acts". Two identical carbon-copy typescripts on unlined quarto paper, 22 sheets, with brown wrapping-paper cover. Handwritten title on the cover reads "*Karaghiozis, Alexander, and the Dreadful Dragon*". Dated July 1980 on the title sheet. Manuscript corrections in the third draft AT4 are incorporated in the typing, and a word deleted in AT4 is omitted, indicating that this is the fourth and latest of the drafts. AT2/3 used as the basis for the text presented in this volume.

GUIDE TO THE PRONUNCIATION OF NAMES AND TITLES

Suggested pronunciation of the names and titles that occur in the shadow plays is given below, with the stressed syllables in italic bold. Those marked with an asterisk are not, strictly speaking, correct Greek or Turkish pronunciation, but will work better in a performance in English than the correct forms with stress on the final syllable. Syllabic division follows English rather than Greek conventions.

*Bar*ba *Yor*gos
Derve*nag*has
Ef*fen*di
*Fa*timah
Hadjia*va*tis
*Hod*ja, the
Kara*ghio*zis
Kolli*ti*ris
Macha*ra*tos
*Meh*met *A*li
Mike*li*dis
Mor*pho*nios*

*Ni*onios*
*Pa*sha, the
Pav*li*dis
Se*lim*
Stav*ra*kas
*Ta*hir* Bey
*Tri*phos
Tsa*ous*
Vi*zier*, the
*Yus*suf *A*li
Za*fi*ra

FOREWORD

A SHORT STUDY OF THE GREEK POPULAR SHADOW-SHOW

The shadow-show is the great folk spectacle of Greece and, under different forms, of the Balkans, North Africa and most of Asia as far east as China and Indonesia. It is known in the Near East as *Karaghiozi*s or *Karaghioz* from the name of its principal puppet, and is said to have originated in China under the Sung Dynasty (AD 960–1280) or — more probably — much earlier.

In its original form, it consisted of motionless cardboard figures whose black shadows were thrown on an illuminated transparent screen to illustrate the long narratives of the professional storytellers. Gradually the figures became more elaborate; they were jointed and often cut out of brightly coloured parchment or thin leather so as to project coloured shadows.

From China the shadow-show, adapting itself to the literature and customs of various countries, travelled to India, Siam and Java to the south and southeast, and westward to Persia (*Ketchel Pehlevan*, the "Bald Hero") and to Asia Minor and Turkey (*Karagöz*, "Black Eye"). Thence it came to the Balkans and to Greece. Some form of the shadow-show seems to have been known in Greece as far back as the fourteenth century, during the long decline of the Byzantine Empire; but it took on its present-day form towards the middle of the nineteenth century, thanks especially to the adaptations of the puppeteers Barbayannis Vrachalis, Yannis Kondos and Dimitrios Mimaros.

It is an interesting point that, when the Sultan of Turkey, Suleyman II, sent an embassy to Louis XIV of France, a shadow-show was included in the ambassador's suite and seems to have attracted the attention of the great satirist, Molière. It is possible that the latter borrowed from it the plot of one of his best-known comedies, *Le médecin malgré lui* (*Doctor in spite of himself*), which, in its original form, is played as *Doctor Karaghiozis* to this day, as Professor Louis Rousel argued in *Karagheuz ou un théâtre d'ombres à Athènes* (Athens, 1921). Professor Roussel even points out that the plot of *Doctor Karaghiozis* contains an added subtlety which is not present in Molière: Karaghiozis revenges himself on his accomplice, Hadjiavatis, by playing his own trick back on him. Roussel concludes his study with the words: "We do not know where our tales originally came from, and there is no proof that, long before Molière, the Turks were not enjoying in the depth of their Asia, their own plays of a *Médecin malgré lui*."

Some general details concerning the shadow-show may be of interest. The stage usually consists of a wooden frame supporting a screen of white calico, twelve-to-fifteen feet (3.6–4.5m) long by about four feet (1.2m) high, which is raised some five feet (1.5m) above the ground. The space beneath the screen is backed by some opaque material to conceal the puppet manipulators, and a kind of shelf runs its whole length, on which the figures for the coming show are placed ready to hand.

These figures, cut out of various stiff materials, cannot, strictly speaking, be termed "puppets" as they are flat and only their profile shadows are meant to appear on the screen. The smaller ones are of thick cardboard and unjointed or only made to bend at the waist. The more important figures, constructed of plywood and coloured parchment, are sometimes real works of art in all the intricate details of their bright oriental costumes. Curiously enough, however, the heads and faces, especially those of the women, are often rather crude and primitive and too big for the sizes of the bodies. This is perhaps unavoidable: the shadows of heads and features of normal proportions would appear too small on the screen.

Most of the larger figures are jointed at the neck, shoulder, waist and knee. Karaghiozis himself has an inordinately long and multi-jointed right arm and hand which comes in particularly useful during his orchard-robbing, shop-lifting and burgling escapades. In the North African shadow-show this arm is replaced by a very different member as, in those countries, the performances are of a coarser character.

The shadow-show betrays its oriental origin by its fidelity to the convention that the more important a person is socially, the bigger he should be represented. Karaghiozis is no exception to this rule: though the principal figure in the cast, he is only of medium size as he is a hunchback of humble social status.

The screen is illuminated from behind by a row of lamps about five feet (1.5m) distant. The figures are flat against the cloth and are "animated" by long wooden rods fixed to the bodies and arms. These rods are manipulated with wonderful dexterity by the showmen, who also imitate the various voices, both male and female, and produce all the necessary sounds from cock-crows to the rumble of distant thunder. The rods, being at right-angles to the plane of the screen, are seen from the front as vague streaks moving around the figures, and are unobtrusive enough to be disregarded. This is an improvement on the Far-Eastern pattern, where the rods are in the same plane as the puppets and consequently cast very obvious shadows.

There is generally little in the way of "stage scenery", but that little often shows great intricacy of design. In most cases the scenery consists simply of the shadow of Karaghiozis' tumble-down hut in the left-hand corner and the elaborate and often beautifully carved and fretted palace of the Vizier on the right.

The plays acted in the Greek shadow-show fall into two classes: the more modern, and the strictly traditional which have a long history behind them. The latter are more popular with most audiences. The shadow-plays enjoy some of the privileges accorded to Aristophanes and the satirists of Ancient Greece. The showmen can introduce scenes and characters of their own invention and "guy" the Mighty and their shortcomings with an outspokenness that no other medium would dare to employ.

―――― o ――――

FOREWORD : A SHORT STUDY OF THE GREEK POPULAR SHADOW-SHOW

Some of the principal puppets of the Greek shadow-show are the following:–

KARAGHIOZIS himself, a bald-headed hunchback with an outsize nose and the hyperflexible arm already mentioned. He is continually getting in and out of scrapes and perpetrating the most outrageous swindles; but he is an ageing rogue and always remains likeable in spite of his moral blemishes.

KOLLITIRIS, the son of Karaghiozis, a tiny replica of his father in looks and roguery.

BARBA YORGOS, a shepherd from the mountains in white pleated *foustanella* (kilt) and tasselled fez. Shrewd and yet naive, he is forever being victimised by his plausible nephew, Karaghiozis. Barba Yorgos, though a simple shepherd, is shown as one of the largest figures, to symbolise his great strength and courage.

HADJIAVATIS, a town-crier by trade, the accomplice and butt of Karaghiozis.

Besides the above, various dignitaries of the old Ottoman Empire are represented: THE VIZIER, THE VALI, THE KHADI and their families, together with Turkish soldiers and the dour Albanian watchman, DERVENAGHAS, from whom Karaghiozis receives many a clout.

There are also typical figures from the different regions of the Balkans. These include KAPETAN NIKOLOS, the sturdy old Hydriote sea-dog who, when riding a donkey, insists on conning it to starboard or to port; STAVRAKAS, the bragging tough from the Piraeus docks; SIOR NIONIOS, the down-at-heel Zantiote aristocrat, always dressed in a seedy tail-coat and a huge top hat.

In some plays ALEXANDER THE GREAT (or ANTIOCHUS) appears in full martial panoply of crested helmet, shield and spear.

On the female side there is a profusion of princesses, witches, sirens; and finally a glut of domestic animals, dragons, sea-monsters, angels, devils, skeletons — more than enough to populate every corner of earth, heaven and hell. Some of these latter, such as the dragons, have many joints and can be made to crawl and writhe in a realistic and hilarious manner.

An orchestra, composed usually of a violin, a guitar, a clarinet and a *daouli* (a kind of barrel-shaped drum), is an important part of the shadow-show. Each figure is heralded by its own distinctive "signature tune" before appearing on the screen. Thus, as Roussel points out, Karaghiozis has anticipated Wagner's leitmotivs by many centuries.

——— o ———

I chose *Doctor Karaghiozis* — an example of a traditional play — as it is interesting to compare the handling of the same theme by both East and West. Neither this nor either of the other two plays that follow has been translated from the script of any single puppeteer. The translations represent a combination of many versions seen by myself, mostly between the years 1920 and 1940, in Athens, Thessaloniki, Yannina, Adrianoupolis and Corfu. I have tried, as much as possible, to reproduce the spirit and atmosphere of the plays, with their quaint blending of Past and Present, and of East and West. Occasionally some untranslatable humorous incident or pun has been replaced by an English equivalent to avoid the distraction of too many references and footnotes.

All three plays in this volume end, in a manner typical of so many of the shadow-plays, with a fight between Karaghiozis and his friend Hadjiavatis — usually over something of no practical importance to either of them. The "curtain goes down" with them rolling off the "stage" locked in combat, with their yells and the thuds of their blows "dying away in the distance". The audience's expectation of this ending is explicitly referred to in the closing lines of *Karaghiozis, Alexander the Great, and the Dreadful Dragon.*

THEODORE STEPHANIDES
LONDON, 1978

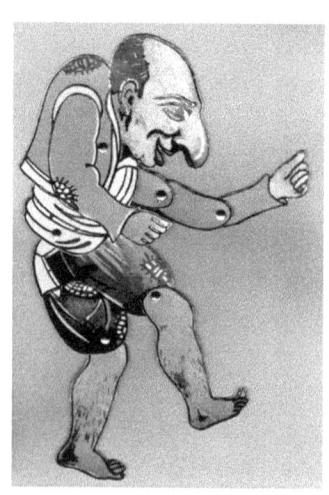

DOCTOR KARAGHIOZIS

Fatimah

Selim

DOCTOR KARAGHIOZIS

PERSONS

KARAGHIOZIS	an engaging and happy-go-lucky hunchback who lives by his wits
HADJIAVATIS	the local town-crier, friend and accomplice of Karaghiozis
KOLLITIRIS	Karaghiozis' small son, a minute replica of his father
THE BEY	a Turkish notable
SELIM	the Bey's son
THE VIZIER	the local Turkish Governor
FATIMAH	the Vizier's daughter
BARBA YORGOS	a mountain shepherd, Karaghiozis' uncle
DERVENAGHAS	the Bey's Albanian door-keeper
SIOR NIONIOS	a middle-aged impoverished dandy from Zante

The scene remains the same during all three Acts. THE BEY'S *mansion is shown on the right-hand side of the screen, and* KARAGHIOZIS' *tumble-down hut on the left.*

ACT ONE

SCENE ONE

HADJIAVATIS (*entering from the right, singing*):
  Orange blossom sweet and fair,
    scent not so the evening air;
  hide your petals from my sight
    lest I linger all the night!
  What then? Wherefore leave so soon?
    Greet with me the rising moon . . .
  As we watch it round and clear,
    you can whisper in my ear.
THE BEY (*entering from the right*): You seem to be in a tuneful mood, my good Hadjiavatis!
HADJIAVATIS (*bowing to the ground*): What would you, Your Honour? I sing though I've long forgotten the tune of two silver sixpences clinked together.
THE BEY: You may be poor, but you've good health. And that's a thing that even my money can't buy.
HADJIAVATIS: Then you are ill, Your Honour?
THE BEY: No, Hadjiavatis, I'm alright; it's my poor son who's ill. I'm half-mad with worry. I've been to all the doctors for miles around, but they can't do anything. My son's melting away like a lighted candle. He'll soon be in his grave if this goes on.
HADJIAVATIS: May I take the liberty of advising Your Honour?
THE BEY: Speak, my good Hadjiavatis; I am ready to listen to anybody if it'll only save my son.
HADJIAVATIS: Your Honour has only consulted *local* doctors. Doctors who haven't studied in any of the great

universities. Why don't you consult a really famous doctor, a Professor, someone with half the alphabet running after his name.

THE BEY: Your advice is excellent, my good Hadjiavatis, but where can I find a famous doctor in a small place like this? And, rich though I am, I can't afford to bring one all the way from London, Paris or Vienna.

HADJIAVATIS: I think, Your Honour, that I could find you the very man you want. A genuine Professor of the University of London Bridge! The Olympic record-holder for the discovery of new diseases! Why, he has to climb a stepladder to pin on all his medals!

THE BEY: Allah be praised! My son may yet be brought back to health. Go, my good Hadjiavatis, fetch me that great doctor and I'll reward you handsomely.

HADJIAVATIS: Have confidence in me, Your Honour. I'll bring him without fail.

(*Exeunt in opposite directions.*)

SCENE TWO

HADJIAVATIS (*shouting outside* KARAGHIOZIS' *hut*): Hi, Karaghiozis!

KARAGHIOZIS (*from inside*): Not at home!

HADJIAVATIS: But I recognise your voice.

KARAGHIOZIS: Well I can't come anyway; I'm asleep.

HADJIAVATIS: You can't be. You're talking.

KARAGHIOZIS: Can't I talk in my sleep without your permission?

HADJIAVATIS: But, Karaghiozis, I've something very important to tell you. Do please come out.

KARAGHIOZIS: Not for all the gold in the world!

HADJIAVATIS (*as if to himself*): Hullo! What's this I've just found? Why, bless my soul, it's a gold watch!
KARAGHIOZIS (*dashing out*): It must be the one I lost yesterday. Hand it over quick!
HADJIAVATIS (*laughing*): There isn't any gold watch. I just said that to make you come out.
KARAGHIOZIS: For two pins I'd give you something to make you go in . . . into hospital for a month!
HADJIAVATIS: Now listen, Karaghiozis: you remember that English doctor who was here a year or two ago collecting microbes?
KARAGHIOZIS: Yes, the microbes collected *him*.
HADJIAVATIS: Can you tell me where he lives?
KARAGHIOZIS: He doesn't live anywhere — he's dead.
HADJIAVATIS: Dead!
KARAGHIOZIS: Yes, he thought he could ride a mule. The mule thought otherwise. He died the year before last. I saw him last year for the last time.
HADJIAVATIS: Impossible, Karaghiozis! You couldn't have seen him *last* year if he died the year *before* last.
KARAGHIOZIS: Yes, I did. He died on December the 31st of the year before last. I saw him on the 1st of January of last year when I helped to coffinate him.
HADJIAVATIS: That's most unfortunate. The Bey promised me a good reward if I could bring him a doctor from some great university. But wait . . . I've got an idea . . . The Bey hasn't been long in these parts, Karaghiozis, he doesn't know you . . .
KARAGHIOZIS: And so what?
HADJIAVATIS: Look! I'll introduce you to the Bey as a London Professor of Medicine, and we'll go shares in whatever he pays me. He'll pay well . . .
KARAGHIOZIS: Yes, in hard cash — with my back as

official receiver! No, no, Hadjiavatis, I've joined you in too many of your wonderful schemes. My back still tingles from the last one. You won't drag me into any more of them.

HADJIAVATIS: But, Karaghiozis, this time . . .

KARAGHIOZIS (*decidedly*): There ain't going to be no this time!

(KARAGHIOZIS *dives back into his hut and slams the door.* HADJIAVATIS *departs disconsolately.*)

SCENE THREE

HADJIAVATIS (*entering left, to himself*): Karaghiozis is in one of his stubborn moods. And I can't do anything without his help . . . But here comes the Bey. Perhaps I can manage things somehow.

THE BEY (*coming out of his mansion*): Ah, my good Hadjiavatis, anything to tell me? Have you found the great English doctor?

HADJIAVATIS (*with many deep bows*): I have, Your Honour. But he absolutely refuses to come here.

THE BEY (*astonished*): Refuses to come! But why, Hadjiavatis?

HADJIAVATIS: Ah, I see that Your Honour has never heard of the great Professor Karaghiozis of the University of London Bridge, the most eccentric character in the medical profession. He goes about dressed in rags and absolutely refuses even to look at a patient. In fact he pretends that he isn't a doctor at all.

THE BEY: But why, why?

HADJIAVATIS: It's unbelievable, Your Honour, but it's so. The greatest medical genius of all the ages, yet he'll look you straight in the eye and tell you that he isn't a doctor and never was one. *He* — with so many diplomas that he needs a special corps of diplomats to keep the moths out of them!

THE BEY: Isn't there *any* way of forcing him to admit that he *is* a doctor?

HADJIAVATIS: There's but one way, Your Honour. By attacking his weak spot. Professor Karaghiozis suffers from xylophobia.

THE BEY: Xylophobia! What's that?

HADJIAVATIS: An inordinate horror of wood . . . if applied with sufficient vigour. Professor Karaghiozis will do anything rather than be subjected to this ordeal. He will even admit that he is a doctor if the contact be sufficiently prolonged.

THE BEY: In that case, my good Hadjiavatis, the problem is solved. My factotum, Dervenaghas, is an expert wood-wielder. No xylophobe is likely to resist his administrations for any length of time. Just persuade Professor Karaghiozis to come here and I'll undertake to prove to him that he's a doctor whether he denies it or not.

HADJIAVATIS: I'll bring him, Your Honour, even if he has to half-kill me.

(*Exeunt in opposite directions.*)

SCENE FOUR

HADJIAVATIS (*approaching* KARAGHIOZIS' *hut*): Hi, Karaghiozis!

KARAGHIOZIS (*appearing from inside*): What's it this time? Found another gold watch?

HADJIAVATIS: The Bey wishes to see you.

KARAGHIOZIS: Well he can go on wishing.

HADJIAVATIS: He's made a bet with the Vizier that you can't eat a hundred and fifty doughnuts at one sitting.

KARAGHIOZIS: I hope they're man-sized ones, not the mingy little things you get at Macharatos in Stadium Street. And did he say anything about standing me a good square meal afterwards for my trouble?

HADJIAVATIS: Yes, Karaghiozis. Lamb pilaffe, egg-plant pie and fig-pudding.

KARAGHIOZIS (*ecstatically*): Lamb pilaffe! Egg-plant pie! Fig-pudding! What are we waiting for, Hadjiavatis? Lead me to them!

(*They cross over to the mansion just as* THE BEY *appears.*)

HADJIAVATIS (*bowing to the ground*): This is the famous Professor Karaghiozis, Your Honour.

KARAGHIOZIS (*thinking it all a joke*): Yes, Professor Karaghiozis, of the great *de* Karaghiozis family. My famous ancestor, the Duke of Karaghiozis, won the Battle of Waterloo for the British by leading a charge of French Grenadiers . . .

THE BEY (*interrupting*): *British* Grenadiers you mean, surely.

KARAGHIOZIS: No, no, *French* Grenadiers. He led the charge backwards instead of forwards.

THE BEY (*to* HADJIAVATIS): You have done well, my good Hadjiavatis. And now pray leave us. I wish to speak to Professor Karaghiozis in private.

HADJIAVATIS (*with many bows*): I go, Your Honour. And may the Grace of Allah surround you. (*Exit*)

THE BEY (*to* KARAGHIOZIS): Professor Karaghiozis, I know all about you. I know that you're a famous doctor . . .

KARAGHIOZIS (*interrupting*): Me a doctor! Never was a

doctor in my life. Why, I don't know one end of an enema from the other!

THE BEY: Come, come, my dear Professor. I said that I knew *all* about you. Surely you'll admit you're a doctor without forcing me to extremes.

KARAGHIOZIS: But how can I admit that I'm a doctor when I'm not one!

THE BEY (*shouting*): Ho, Dervenaghas, come here!

(DERVENAGHAS *appears with a big stick.*) Now, my dear Professor, are you a doctor or not?

KARAGHIOZIS: What's all this? I don't understand! I tell you I'm not a doctor and never was one.

THE BEY: Dervenaghas, just treat the Professor to a little superficial massage.

(DERVENAGHAS *obeys with enthusiasm.*)

KARAGHIOZIS: Ow, ouch, ow! Stop, stop!

THE BEY (*inexorably*): Are you a doctor? Yes or no!

KARAGHIOZIS: No, ouch, not yet. But I'm beginning to be one. Ouch, I feel it in my bones!

THE BEY: Dervenaghas, a little vibratory friction!

KARAGHIOZIS: Ow, ouch, stop! I *am* a doctor now. My diploma's stamped all over me in black and blue.

THE BEY: Ah, I knew that, if I tried hard enough, I'd persuade you to remember that you're the most famous doctor in the whole world. And now to business: when you've cured my dear son, Selim, I'll pay you one hundred pounds.

KARAGHIOZIS: Plus one-and-fourpence for my bus fare.

THE BEY: One hundred pounds, one shilling and four pence, agreed. And now will you come and see your patient?

KARAGHIOZIS (*shocked*): Now? Good heavens, no! How could I cure anyone in these clothes! I must get my morning coat, my sponge-bag trousers and my top hat. The fate of the patient may depend on them! A question of life or death!

THE BEY (*much impressed*): All right, my dear Professor; you know what's best for the patient. I'll wait for you here with Selim in half an hour.

(*Exeunt in opposite directions.*)

ACT TWO

SCENE ONE

KARAGHIOZIS (*shouting inside his hut*): Kollitiris!

KOLLITIRIS: Yes, fadler.

KARAGHIOZIS: Where's the morning coat I stole from the rag-and-bone merchant?

KOLLITIRIS: Pussy's having kittens on it, fadler.

KARAGHIOZIS: Well, turn her off then and bring it here. Together with the sponge-bag trousers we got off that scarecrow.

KOLLITIRIS: Yes, fadler.

KARAGHIOZIS (*indignantly*): Hey! Where's the other trouser leg?

KOLLITIRIS: Mummy's cleaning the saucepans with it, fadler.

KARAGHIOZIS: Tell her to sew it on again at once. The idea of cleaning the saucepans with a perfectly new old pair of trousers that even a marquis wouldn't wear! What are women coming to nowadays! Yes, and bring me my patent ventilated top hat; the one with a hole in the crown. Guaranteed to prevent apoplexy by supplying a down-draught to cool the brain.

KOLLITIRIS: Yes, fadler.

KARAGHIOZIS (*appearing outside his hut*): Ah, here we are, all dressed up as a Professor of the famous University of London Bridge should be: top hat, morning coat, sponge-bag trousers, *and* spats. Pity that I couldn't steal a pair of shoes to go with them; but I'll persuade the Bey that going barefoot is the latest London health craze. *All* the celebrities are doing it. But what's that I hear! A buzz-saw mated to a steam siren?

SIOR NIONIOS (*entering from the right, singing*):
> O Zante, fairest of all isles,
>> could you but larger be!
>
> For all your houses, big and small,
>> are crowded by the sea.
>
> They go and blame my pussy-cat
>> and say that she is old;
>
> her tail is white, her eyes are blue,
>> her nose is pink and cold.

KARAGHIOZIS (*laughing*): It's Nionios, that addle-pated serenader again. He'd flirt with a brick wall if it was dressed in petticoats!

SIOR NIONIOS (*recoiling in surprise*): The saints preserve us! What do I see? Karaghiozis all dressed up like a lord!

KARAGHIOZIS: And why not, you Zantiote* yokel? A Professor of the great University of London Bridge must dress as becomes his station.

SIOR NIONIOS: You a Professor!

KARAGHIOZIS: Yes, I was awarded my diploma this morning. Have a look at my back if you don't believe me.

SIOR NIONIOS: Well, I wish you could cure me from what *I'm* suffering from.

KARAGHIOZIS: Perhaps I might. What are you suffering from, Sior Nionios?

SIOR NIONIOS: Love, my dear Karaghiozis, love! I'm in love with Fatimah, the Vizier's daughter.

KARAGHIOZIS: Bouncing brick-bats! And does she return your love?

SIOR NIONIOS: Alas, no! She secretly loves another. In fact she's ill with longing; she's wasting away like a lighted candle. The Vizier's half-mad with worry. He's brought in shoals of doctors and none of them can diagnose her complaint.

KARAGHIOZIS: And how do *you* know all this?

SIOR NIONIOS: Well, whilst I was hanging around after Fatimah, I . . . er . . . had a little affair with her maid . . .

KARAGHIOZIS: I see. When we can't have the caviar, we reach for the bloater-paste, eh?

SIOR NIONIOS: . . . and the maid told me about Fatimah's illness. I guessed the reason because of my own love for her. It takes a lover to see through a lover, you know.

KARAGHIOZIS: And have you guessed whom she loves?

SIOR NIONIOS: No, Karaghiozis. But I know she's dying of love for someone. *That's* certain.

KARAGHIOZIS: Thank you, Sior Nionios. What you've told me may be very important. I must think this over very carefully. And now good day to you.

SIOR NIONIOS: And good day to you, my dear Karaghiozis.

(*Exeunt in opposite directions.*)

SCENE TWO

THE BEY (*coming out of his mansion, to* KARAGHIOZIS, *entering left*): Ah, my dear Professor Karaghiozis, how pleased I am to see you again! Here is my son, Selim, whom I expect you to cure.

KARAGHIOZIS: And so this is Selim! What's your trouble, my young man?

(*He is answered only by a sigh and a blank stare.*)

THE BEY: You won't get anything out of him, I'm afraid. He's been like that for the last month. He neither talks nor eats; just moons about and sighs as if his wits had deserted him.

KARAGHIOZIS: Perhaps he had none in the first place. But tell me, my dear Bey, have you tried varying his diet?

THE BEY: We've tried all the choicest foods: stuffed peacock; quails' breasts in aspic; nightingales' tongues . . .

KARAGHIOZIS (*with absorbed interest*): Tripe and onions? Fish and chips? Sausages and mash? What the lad needs is something really substantial, something to brace up his stomach like a scaffolding pole. Have you tried him with a good heaped-up plate of boiled salt cod surrounded with half a peck of turnips, and tomatoes, and potatoes, and . . .

THE BEY (*interrupting*): We've tried everything, Professor, but he just throws it all away.

KARAGHIOZIS (*scandalised*): Throws it all away! The tripe in aspic! The cods' breasts! The nightingales' tongues and mash! Where, where? Tell me and I'll get Kollitiris to stand guard with a dinner-pail.

THE BEY (*stiffly*): My dear Professor, aren't you ever going to examine the patient?

KARAGHIOZIS: What patient? Oh, ah, yes. Of course, yes. (*To* SELIM): Open your mouth and close your eyes. Now open your eyes and close your mouth, and now let me feel your pulse and your pocket-book. Hum, ha, yes. Hum . . .

THE BEY (*anxiously*): Can you name his disease, Professor Karaghiozis?

KARAGHIOZIS (*gravely*): It's a disease that has no name. So far, the patient has always died before its name could be discovered.

THE BEY (*horrified*): Oh, my poor son! Is he in such danger?

KARAGHIOZIS: He is in immortal danger. The disease is

always two hundred per cent fatal!

THE BEY: Two hundred per cent! But that's impossible. It can't be more than one hundred per cent.

KARAGHIOZIS: No, no, two hundred per cent. Statistics show that a hundred people contract this disease every year. They *all* die: that makes one hundred per cent. But another hundred, who *haven't* got the disease, die of fright because they *think* they've got it. That makes two hundred per cent, exactly as I told you.

THE BEY: Oh, my poor, poor Selim! Can nothing save him?

KARAGHIOZIS (*to himself, after another look at* SELIM): Now where have I seen that dying-duck expression before? Wasn't it on the face of our good Sior Nionios? Ha, I have an idea. (*Aloud*): Have courage, my dear Bey, nothing is impossible to a Professor of the University of Xylophagy* like myself. But I would like to examine the patient once more in private.

THE BEY: Certainly, Professor. I'll leave you both together. And may Allah quicken your insight. (*Exit.*)

KARAGHIOZIS (*slapping* SELIM *on the back*): Ha, ha, Selim, my boy! I think that I *can* give a name to your disease: Love! You're in love with Fatimah, the Vizier's daughter.

SELIM (*startled out of his apathy*): By Allah, Professor Karaghiozis, you must be a wizard! You not only name my disease, but also the object of my devotion!

KARAGHIOZIS: Tut, tut! Us Professors of Medicine are so used to diagnosing the names of complicated diseases, that diagnosing the name of a girl is mere child's play. But tell me, my good Selim, what would you give to be united to your beloved Fatimah?

SELIM (*fervently*): I would give my heart's blood!

KARAGHIOZIS: And what the dickens would I do with

your heart's blood? But would you give fifty pounds? Plus one-and-fourpence for my bus fare?

SELIM: I would give them gladly. But I'm afraid that your efforts will be in vain. The Vizier would never condescend to give his daughter to the son of a mere Bey. Why, he has refused Pashas and Princes!

KARAGHIOZIS: Listen to me, Selim me lad. Do everything I tell you and all will be well. Just continue as you were, moping and sighing and refusing to speak or eat, until I give you one of my potions. Then you must return to normal with a bang! Do this and I guarantee that you will be hugging your beloved Fatimah within the week.

SELIM: It shall be done as you say.

(*Exeunt in opposite directions.*)

SCENE THREE

THE BEY (*coming out of his mansion, to* KARAGHIOZIS, *entering left*): Ah, my dear Professor Karaghiozis, have you any good news for me? Is there any hope for my poor Selim?

KARAGHIOZIS: He will most certainly be cured if he drinks the potion I have written down in this prescription. (*He hands* THE BEY *a paper covered with meaningless markings.*)

THE BEY (*snatching it eagerly*): May Allah reward you!

KARAGHIOZIS: And may *you* reward me also! But hold hard a minute — where are you going?

THE BEY: I'm hurrying to the chemist's shop to have your prescription made up.

KARAGHIOZIS (*in horrified tones*): Good gracious, my dear Bey! Did you think that any *ordinary* chemist could make up *my* prescriptions? No, no, there is only one chemist in all the world who has my full confidence!

THE BEY (*much impressed*): And who is he?

KARAGHIOZIS: The most marvellous chemist, physicist, taxidermist, bicyclist, bigamist that ever was! It was he who deciphered the Rosetta Stone by comparing it to an Income Tax form! It was he who shouted "Eureka" after splitting the atom in his bath!

THE BEY: Pray tell me the name of this paragon and I'll send for him at once.

KARAGHIOZIS (*to himself*): Ha, ha, Hadjiavatis my boy, here's where I'll get a bit of my own back! (*Aloud*): You already know him: Hadjiavatis.

THE BEY (*astonished*): Hadjiavatis! But he's not a chemist! He's only the town-crier and man-of-all-work.

KARAGHIOZIS: That's what *he* says. But he's really the best chemist in all the world. His diplomas fill a whole vault in the National Bank!

THE BEY: But why should he conceal the fact?

KARAGHIOZIS: Oh, just a little eccentricity on his part. We great men, you know, we all have a screw loose somewhere. But I'll tell you a secret: he too suffers from xylophobia like myself. In fact it was from him that I caught the disease during the course of our long association. *Xylophobia*, you understand. Need I say more?

THE BEY: No, no, my dear Professor, the needful shall be done. My man Dervenaghas, as you yourself know, has a persuasive touch. Bring me Hadjiavatis and he'll soon admit that he's a chemist.

KARAGHIOZIS: Right, my dear Bey! Expect us both here in ten minutes.

(*Exeunt in opposite directions.*)

SCENE FOUR

HADJIAVATIS (*entering from the right, singing*):
>Mine was the fault, I must confess,
>>Ah, never was such bashfulness!
>
>Behind the hedgerow we did meet,
>>Yet I kissed not her lips so sweet,
>
>Alas! Alas! Alas!

KARAGHIOZIS (*entering from the left*): Hi, Hadjiavatis, the Bey wants to pay you the reward he promised you.

HADJIAVATIS: Good! Let's go to him. I wonder how much he'll give me.

KARAGHIOZIS: A good bit more than you expect! I can tell you that.

HADJIAVATIS: That's splendid news, Karaghiozis! They say he's a generous man.

KARAGHIOZIS: Yes, as generous with his wood as Croesus with his gold. He'll bankrupt himself one of these days if our backs hold out.

HADJIAVATIS: Perhaps he'll give me ten pounds. I wonder if I dare ask for more.

KARAGHIOZIS: Quite unnecessary, Hadjiavatis my boy. You'll soon be getting so many pounds that you'll be yelling "enough!".

HADJIAVATIS: Oh, I'm all impatience. There's the Bey outside his mansion; let's hurry!

THE BEY (*to* HADJIAVATIS): Welcome, my dear Mister Hadjiavatis, I'm so pleased you've been able to come. I have a little prescription for you to make up.

HADJIAVATIS (*looking at the paper with bewilderment*): What's this, Your Honour? How am I to make up a prescription!

THE BEY: Come, come, Mister Hadjiavatis, I know *all* about you. I know that you're the most famous chemist in the world. It's useless to deny it.

HADJIAVATIS: *Me* a chemist, Your Honour! Who could have told Your Honour such a thing!

THE BEY: Professor Karaghiozis told me when he wrote out this prescription. He told me also that he always had *you* to make them up.

HADJIAVATIS: But Karaghiozis can't even write, Your Honour, and anyway I can't read.

THE BEY: Neither can Doctor Pavlidis of Stadium Street (who is looking at us from a front seat) nor the chemist on Omonia Square, but between them both they see to it that the patient gets his bottle of coloured water. And now, Mister Hadjiavatis, will you make up this prescription; yes or no?

HADJIAVATIS: But I can't, Your Honour! I tell you that I'm not a chemist and never was one!

THE BEY: Ho there, Dervenaghas, give Mister Hadjiavatis a touch of your persuader!

DERVENAGHAS (*appearing*): Poh yah, Master, me touch him up good and proper!

HADJIAVATIS: Ow, ouch, stop, stop!

THE BEY: Are you a chemist; yes or no?

KARAGHIOZIS (*gleefully*): Tickle him up a bit more, Dervenaghas, he hasn't *quite* got his diploma yet!

HADJIAVATIS: Ow, ouch, stop! Yes, I'm a chemist! I'm a chemist!

THE BEY: Ah, my dear Mister Hadjiavatis, I thought I'd persuade you in the end to admit your high qualifications. And now please make up this prescription. My son Selim is waiting to be cured.

HADJIAVATIS (*to himself*): In for a penny, in for a pound. I'll just invent a potion of sorts and it'll be up to the patient to survive it. (*Aloud, pretending to read*): Ah yes, quinine ten thousand minims; castor oil a pint; prussic acid fourteen scruples; denationalised alcohol twelve ounces; best red ink *ad lib*. A tumbler-full to be taken every fifteen minutes until cure or death. Yes, Your Honour, I'll make up this potion with the greatest skill and care and bring it back here in half an hour. (*Exit left.* THE BEY *and* KARAGHIOZIS *exeunt right.*)

SCENE FIVE

THE BEY (*coming out of his mansion*): The half-hour is almost up ... Ah, here comes Professor Karaghiozis with the medicine. My dear Selim will soon be well.

KARAGHIOZIS (*entering with a bottle almost as big as himself*): Greetings, my dear Bey, and where's Selim? It's time for his first dose.

THE BEY: Selim, Selim, Professor Karaghiozis has brought your medicine. Come, my dear son, and be made well again.

(SELIM *appears.*)

KARAGHIOZIS (*handing* SELIM *the bottle*): Now, my good Selim, drink your medicine and be cured.

(SELIM *takes a sniff and puts the bottle down with a shake of his head.*)

THE BEY (*persuasively*): Drink your medicine, my son.

(SELIM *again shakes his head.*)

KARAGHIOZIS: Leave me alone with the patient, my dear Bey, and I think I'll be able to persuade him.

(THE BEY *goes out.*)

SELIM (*indignantly*): What's this muck you want me to drink, Professor? It smells like bilge water!

KARAGHIOZIS: And it probably is! But don't you love

Fatimah?

SELIM (*ecstatically*): Ah, for her sake I'd attack dragons with my bare hands! I'd go through hell and high water! I'd . . .

KARAGHIOZIS (*interrupting*): And yet you refuse to drink a little medicine. Just a teeny weeny bottle of delicious medicine.

SELIM: That's different. I said I'd go through hell and high water — not *drink* them!

KARAGHIOZIS: Come, come, my dear Selim, you're upsetting all my plans. When the Bey comes back, just drink one mouthful from this bottle, one little sip. And then start talking . . .

SELIM: You bet I'll start talking! . . . if I'm still alive.

THE BEY (*appearing again*): Have you persuaded him, my dear Professor?

KARAGHIOZIS: I have, my dear Bey. Master Selim will now oblige . . .

(SELIM *takes a cautious sip.*)

SELIM (*coughing and spluttering*): Pouah, ugh, help! I'm choking! I'm dying! Bring me wine, quick!

THE BEY (*delighted*): A miracle, my dear Professor! It's the first time my beloved son has spoken for weeks. And see: the red has come back to his cheeks — he looks another man!

SELIM (*still spluttering*): And I *feel* another man too, but not the one I'd have chosen to be. I won't get this filthy taste out of my mouth for a twelve-month! And, good heavens! The castor oil . . . (*He rushes out.*)

THE BEY: How can I thank you enough, Professor Karaghiozis! Come in and have a coffee while I count out your fee.

(*They enter the mansion together.*)

ACT THREE

SCENE ONE

HADJIAVATIS (*knocking on the door of* KARAGHIOZIS' *hut*): Hi, Karaghiozis, great news! The Vizier himself wants to see you! He's waiting for you at the Bey's mansion.

KARAGHIOZIS: Hum, I think I can guess why. Hadjiavatis my boy, we'll both be millionaires before the week's out! (KARAGHIOZIS *crosses over to* THE BEY'S *mansion where he is met by* THE VIZIER.)

THE VIZIER: Professor Karaghiozis, I've just heard from my friend, the Bey, of your wonderful cure of his son Selim. You can do me a similar favour: my daughter Fatimah is suffering from a disease which has also baffled the doctors for miles around. Cure her and you shall earn my eternal gratitude.

KARAGHIOZIS: And what, my dear Vizier, is the equivalent of your eternal gratitude in L.S.D.?*

THE VIZIER: Will two hundred pounds be enough?

KARAGHIOZIS: No. I must also have one-and-fourpence for my bus fare.

THE VIZIER: Two hundred pounds, one shilling and four pence it shall be.

KARAGHIOZIS: Right ho! Fetch your daughter and I'll vet her straight away.

THE VIZIER (*calling over his shoulder*): Hi, Dervenaghas!

KARAGHIOZIS (*backing away hastily*): Hola, my dear Vizier, I've already had my diploma. I don't need another for this job.

THE VIZIER: I don't understand you, Professor. I only

want Dervenaghas to go and fetch Fatimah.
KARAGHIOZIS: That's all right then. So long as it's not to distribute diplomas. He awards them with rather a heavy hand.
DERVENAGHAS (*appearing*): Poh yah, Lord Vizier, me come. Me massage Professor?
THE VIZIER: No, no, my good Dervenaghas. I only want you to tell my daughter Fatimah to come here. (DERVENAGHAS *re-enters the house and his voice is heard bawling "Poh yah, Missy Fatimah, your father he say you come down!"* FATIMAH *appears, walking slowly and listlessly.*)
KARAGHIOZIS: Are you in pain, my dear Miss Fatimah? Have you heartburn, flatulence, spots before the eyes, swollen legs, backaches, pimples, piles? Then take Petrucchio's Purple Pills for... Ah no, I read that in the paper this morning...
(FATIMAH'S *only answer is a sigh.*)
THE VIZIER: I'm afraid it's useless questioning her, my dear Professor; nobody can get a word out of her. She's been like that for the last six weeks; sighing and refusing to speak. She won't eat either; she's melting away like a lighted candle, and I'm off my head with worry!
KARAGHIOZIS: Hum, ha, my dear Vizier, I think I recognise those symptoms. Your daughter is suffering from malignant selimitis.*
THE VIZIER (*horrified*): Oh, my poor daughter! Malignant selimitis! It sounds terrible!
KARAGHIOZIS: And it's even more terrible than it sounds! But I would like to talk to your daughter in private so as to confirm the diagnosis.
THE VIZIER: As you wish, my dear Professor.
(*Exit.*)
KARAGHIOZIS: And now, my dear Fatimah, I think I can

tell you what you are really suffering from: love for Selim.

FATIMAH (*startled*): You must be a wizard, Professor Karaghiozis, or how could you have guessed my secret!

KARAGHIOZIS: Ah, ha! Us Professors of the famous University of London Bridge we know our onions and how many beans make fifty-five. We have our methods and we *never* make mistakes.

FATIMAH: You are right, Professor Karaghiozis; I'm dying of love for Selim, but I know that my father would never consent to our union. He wants me to marry a prince or a king.

KARAGHIOZIS: There are ways and means, my dear Fatimah, known only to we Professors of the famous University of London Bridge. But even professors have to live, and a little palm-oil is marvellous for making the world go round. In short, what will there be in it for me if I heave Selim safely into your arms?

FATIMAH: Ah, do that, my dear darling Professor, and I'll give you fifty pounds.

KARAGHIOZIS: No, no, I must have much more. I must also have one-and-fourpence for my bus fare.

FATIMAH: Fifty pounds, one shilling and four pence. Agreed.

KARAGHIOZIS: Good! And now you must promise to do exactly what I tell you.

FATIMAH: I will, my dear Professor, I will! But listen, I have just thought of a plan. My father has full confidence in you; so why not suggest that the one and only way of saving my life would be to marry me to Selim?

KARAGHIOZIS: Pouf! A bit too obvious, my dear Fatimah. Even your father would smell a rat. But leave things to me and I'll arrange it all. Now remember: you must go on being dumb and moonstruck until you hear me say "Prancing pumpkins!" Then, and only then, must you come to your proper senses. If you do so before, all is lost.

FATIMAH: I will do everything exactly as you say, Professor Karaghiozis. And now I must return to my father or he will be getting impatient. We will be expecting you again in half an hour.

(*Exeunt in opposite directions.*)

SCENE TWO

THE VIZIER (*coming out of the Bey's mansion*): Ah, here comes Professor Karaghiozis! My dear Professor, I hope that your diagnosis is not as bad as you first thought.

KARAGHIOZIS (*gravely*): It is even worse. She has *double* selimitis.

THE VIZIER (*horrified*): *Double* selimitis! Allah preserve us! Is there no hope?

KARAGHIOZIS: There is but one hope — and a slender one at that. But the only alternative is a swift and painful death.

THE VIZIER (*wringing his hands*): And what is that? Oh, I will do anything, anything to save my darling Fatimah!

KARAGHIOZIS: Fatimah must marry a shepherd who was born under the same star as herself. The same star within a fraction of an inch.

THE VIZIER (*indignantly*): A shepherd! I would never allow my daughter to marry a shepherd. Why, princes have asked for her hand!

KARAGHIOZIS (*very gravely*): The only alternative is a very horrible and agonising death.

THE VIZIER (*sadly*): In that case I must bow to the will of Allah. But how are we to discover this shepherd?

KARAGHIOZIS: Us Professors of the great University of London Bridge are all stargazers. Our heads are always in the clouds. And we can read the crystal also. Wait a moment and I'll fetch mine.

(KARAGHIOZIS *goes out and returns with a huge bottle labelled "whisky".*)

THE VIZIER: Is that your magic crystal?

KARAGHIOZIS: It is the crystal always used by we Professors of the famous University of London Bridge. After consulting it a few times we can see *anything*.

THE VIZIER: Then quick, my dear Professor, look into it and find this shepherd.

KARAGHIOZIS: If I consult it long enough I shall probably be seeing *two* shepherds!

(KARAGHIOZIS *takes a long swig at the bottle and then stares at it earnestly.*)

THE VIZIER (*anxiously*): Do you see him?

KARAGHIOZIS: I see him, yes I see him: his name is Barba Yorgos and he lives not far from here ... But hullo! What's this? I see another figure too. A young man, quite handsome, but ...

THE VIZIER (*interrupting*): Might this young man not be a more suitable husband than the shepherd?

KARAGHIOZIS: Oh, no, no, no! He was born at least one fiftieth of an inch further from the star's centre of influence. As a remedy for your daughter's disease the shepherd will be much more potent. I insist on the medicine being taken three times per day and sixteen times per night, or I throw up the case.

THE VIZIER: So be it then, Professor Karaghiozis, I bow

to your superior wisdom. Could you bring me this shepherd, Barba Yorgos?

KARAGHIOZIS: I'll bring him here in an hour. Have everything ready for the betrothals.

(*Exeunt in opposite directions.*)

SCENE THREE

KARAGHIOZIS' *hut is seen to be shaking violently. Loud shouts and yells are heard from within.* KARAGHIOZIS *appears from the left and roars through the window.*

KARAGHIOZIS: Barba Yorgos, hi Barba Yorgos! Come out here; I've something important to tell you.

BARBA YORGOS (*coming out of the hut*): Ha, Nephew Karaghiozis! I was romping with that scamp of a grand-nephew of mine, Kollitiris. We had a grand time. He nearly bit my thumb off.

KARAGHIOZIS: Well, Barba Yorgos, the last time you both romped together, you knocked out two of his back teeth.

BARBA YORGOS: I only patted him on the cheek.

KARAGHIOZIS: Oh, I know it was only a play pat — Kollitiris' head was still on his shoulders. But listen, Uncle: Dervenaghas says that your yoghourt tastes like mouldy chalk and that each pint of your milk contains enough water to float the *Queen Mary.**

BARBA YORGOS (*furiously*): Is that what he said, that spindle-shanked son of a sheep-stealer! My delicious yoghourt! My lovely milk! Wait till I get at him, I'll tear him to bits with my bare hands!

KARAGHIOZIS: That's exactly what Dervenaghas said he'd do to you, Uncle. He also said that, if you dared to meet him face to face, you must knock on the door of the Bey's mansion and shout "Fatimah".

BARBA YORGOS (*suspiciously*): Fatimah? Why Fatimah?

KARAGHIOZIS: It's the Albanian for "I accept your challenge. Come outside and I'll knock your ugly head off!"

BARBA YORGOS: That seems a tremendous lot for just one little word!

KARAGHIOZIS: It's often the smallest sausage that contains the most pepper, and the shortest woman who has the longest tongue.

BARBA YORGOS: Tell Dervenaghas that I'll be there in five minutes and that I'll teach him to insult my lovely milk and my delicious yoghourt! Ha, the villain, the misbegotten ape, the squint-eyed sheep-stealer! I'll make him *swallow* the *Queen Mary* when I get my hands on him!

KARAGHIOZIS (*hurrying back to the mansion*): Ha, ha! The air grows sultry. I predict a thunderstorm – with Barba Yorgos' fists for thunderbolts!

(KARAGHIOZIS *enters the mansion. A few minutes later* BARBA YORGOS *appears and starts hammering on the door and roaring "Fatimah!". The whole house rocks.*)

THE VIZIER (*from within*): Oh Professor Karaghiozis, what's this? An earthquake?

KARAGHIOZIS (*from within*): No, no, only its younger brother.

BARBA YORGOS (*shouting and hammering*): Fatimah! Fatimah! Come here, Fatimah, I say! Come out and I'll twist you into a lovers' knot!

KARAGHIOZIS (*from within*): An impetuous lover is he not, my dear Vizier? Just listen to him whispering "Fatimah".

BARBA YORGOS: Fatimah! Fatimah! A thousand devils, can't you hear me calling "Fatimah!"? Are you coming

ACT THREE

out, yes or no?

THE VIZIER (*tremulously, from within*): But this is terrible, Professor Karaghiozis! Can't you go down and tell him to go away?

KARAGHIOZIS (*from within*): What! In his present exalted mood? Why, he'd telegraph me to the chimney pots! He'd send me there by wireless!

BARBA YORGOS (*still louder*): Fatimah! Fatimah! Come out and see what I'll do to you!

KARAGHIOZIS (*from within*): Listen, my dear Vizier, listen to his tender serenade!

THE VIZIER (*from within*): He'll have the whole place down in another minute! Dervenaghas! Dervenaghas! Save us; drive that terrible creature away!

DERVENAGHAS (*from within*): Poh yah, Effendi* Vizier; me drive him, me give him diploma!

(DERVENAGHAS *rushes out and confronts* BARBA YORGOS)

BARBA YORGOS: So there you are at last, you shirking sheep-stealer! I'll teach you to insult my lovely milk, my delicious yoghourt! Come near and I'll tear your tonsils out!

DERVENAGHAS: Poh yah, me give you diploma!

(*A terrific fight takes place.* KARAGHIOZIS *darts out in his excitement and starts distributing kicks and smacks impartially to both combatants. But he gets knocked down in the mêlée and trampled on by the two fighters.*)

KARAGHIOZIS: Ow, ouch! Get off me, you big louts! Do you take my back for a boxing ring or my stomach for the dancing floor of the Hotel Grande Bretagne!

DERVENAGHAS (*shouting with each blow he lands on* BARBA YORGOS): Poh yah, you catch diploma! . . . And triploma! . . . And tetraploma! . . . *And* pentaploma! . . .

BARBA YORGOS (*roaring like a bull and landing twice as many blows*): Ho, mouldy chalk! . . . Ha, *Queen Mary*! . . . Take this . . . and this . . . *And* this! . . .

KARAGHIOZIS (*still struggling to get up*): Let me up, you big brutes! You're ruining the set of my collar! You've spoilt the crease of my trousers! Ow, ouch! . . .
(*The fight continues till* DERVENAGHAS *is finally put to rout and flees, hotly pursued by* BARBA YORGOS.)

SCENE FOUR

KARAGHIOZIS (*entering left, still rubbing himself*): To hell with both those clodhoppers! I'm all black and blue again. And I who thought I'd finished my curriculum!

THE VIZIER (*coming out of the mansion*): Thanks be to Allah, that terrible shepherd is gone. I thought our very last hour had come! And now, my dear Professor, there's nothing to be done except for you to consult your magic crystal again. Find out who is that other young man who can save my daughter by marrying her. At any rate he can't possibly be as dreadful as that Barba Yorgos.

KARAGHIOZIS: No, no, no, my dear Vizier! I beg you to let me go and bring back Barba Yorgos. He may improve on acquaintance.

THE VIZIER: No, by Allah, anything but that! Let us at least see what this other man is like.

KARAGHIOZIS: But, my dear Vizier, he's a little runt of a creature not much taller than yourself. And he couldn't shake this house, not even if he tried with one hand tied behind him.

THE VIZIER: Thank heavens for that, my dear Professor. And now, once again, I beg you to look into your magic crystal.

ACT THREE

KARAGHIOZIS (*reluctantly*): Well, since *you* insist, I'll see what I can do.
(KARAGHIOZIS *fetches the whisky bottle, takes a good drink, and then gazes fixedly at it.*)
THE VIZIER (*anxiously*): Can you see anything, Professor?
KARAGHIOZIS (*gravely*): I see ... yes, I see ... clouds ... only rolling clouds ... Ah, now the clouds dissolve ... I see a young man ... His name is Sel ... Sel ... Seltzer ... Selfridges ... No, now I have it: his name is Selim, and he is the son of your friend, the Bey ...
THE VIZIER (*delighted*): The son of a Bey! Not of a shepherd, or a crossing-sweeper, or a rag-and-bone merchant! Allah be praised! My darling Fatimah can be saved at not too great a cost to her feelings or to my dignity. Professor, Professor, fetch me this admirable youth!
KARAGHIOZIS: I'll have him here before you know I've gone. In the meanwhile trot out your daughter and watch her return to life and health as Selim clasps her in his arms.
(KARAGHIOZIS *goes out and returns with* SELIM. FATIMAH *comes out of the mansion and joins her father.*)
SELIM: Fatimah, my darling Fatimah, speak to me! Come to my arms!
KARAGHIOZIS (*to* THE VIZIER): Now watch the instantaneous cure! See what a Professor of the great University of London *and* Westminster Bridge can do!
SELIM: Fatimah, Fatimah, speak to me!
(FATIMAH *remains dumb and apathetic.*)
KARAGHIOZIS: My goodness! What's wrong now? Has the wretched girl really lost her senses!
SELIM: My darling, my dearest! Won't you put me out of my suspense!

(*There is still no response from* FATIMAH.)

THE VIZIER (*angrily to* KARAGHIOZIS): What's this, Professor Karaghiozis? Didn't you promise me that Fatimah would be cured? Are you a rogue and a cheat?

KARAGHIOZIS (*to himself*): And now for Dervenaghas to administer a few more diplomas! I'll be knighted and beknighted before everything's finished!

SELIM: Fatimah, oh my Fatimah, speak to me or my heart will break!

(*There is still no answer from* FATIMAH.)

KARAGHIOZIS: What's wrong with the silly little fool! Why doesn't she ... But no! It's *me* the fool ... I quite forgot ...

THE VIZIER: What did you forget, Professor Karaghiozis?

KARAGHIOZIS: The word! The stupendous magic word known only to we Professors of the famous University of London Bridge. Now watch: the cure will be instantaneous!

(KARAGHIOZIS *goes up to* FATIMAH *and bellows "Prancing pumpkins!" in her ear.*)

FATIMAH (*falling into* SELIM'S *arms*): Heart of my heart! Oh my beloved!

SELIM (*pressing her to his breast*): Light of my eyes! Darling of my soul!

KARAGHIOZIS: Bless you, my children! Bless you, my bank balance!

THE VIZIER (*amazed*): Professor Karaghiozis, you have my deepest gratitude and admiration!

(*Exeunt all, in opposite directions.*)

ACT THREE

SCENE FIVE

KARAGHIOZIS (*entering left with* HADJIAVATIS): Two hundred lovely little poundlets from the Vizier! A hundred from the Bey! And fifty each from Selim and Fatimah! . . . Four hundred pounds! Oh, Hadjiavatis, we're rich! I didn't know there was that much money in all the world! And then there's the five shillings and four pence I saved in bus fares by riding in my Rolls Royce.

HADJIAVATIS: And don't try to embezzle the ten pounds the Bey gave you to give *me* for having found him such a wonderful doctor! Four hundred and *ten* pounds, five shillings and four pence . . . Trot them out, Karaghiozis me lad, I'm longing to hear 'em clink!

KARAGHIOZIS: I can't show you the money now, Hadjiavatis. I put it all on a horse for the Phaleron races. We'll be *trillionaires* by tonight!

HADJIAVATIS: A horse! You put all our hard-earned money on a horse! Karaghiozis, you wretch, you've ruined us! We'll lose it all!

KARAGHIOZIS (*indignantly*): What do you take me for, Hadjiavatis? I've put it all on a horse which is running at odds of 100 to 1!

HADJIAVATIS: And what does that mean, Karaghiozis?

KARAGHIOZIS: A hundred chances of winning to only one of losing, of course! Would I have chosen that horse otherwise!

HADJIAVATIS: Oh splendid, Karaghiozis! Oh wonderful! I was a fool to doubt you. Hurrah, we'll be *multi*-trillionaires!

KARAGHIOZIS: Yes, and when we get all that money, I'll put my share of it into real estate. No more Government bonds for me!

HADJIAVATIS: But you never *had* any Government bonds.

KARAGHIOZIS: Well, and what difference does that make? Whether I'd had a million Government bonds or none at all, the end result would be the same: I'd have nothing!

HADJIAVATIS: Except that in the first case you'd have something you could sell to the wastepaper merchants.

KARAGHIOZIS: Very true, Hadjiavatis. And that's why I'm going in for real estate this time. I'll buy up *all* the houses in the world.

HADJIAVATIS: Good for you! And I, I'll buy up *all* the furniture in the world.

KARAGHIOZIS: I wouldn't do that, Hadjiavatis. Most of your furniture would get spoilt by the first autumn rains.

HADJIAVATIS: Oh no it wouldn't, Karaghiozis. I'd store it in your houses.

KARAGHIOZIS: Ho! Would you? And what if I refused my permission?

HADJIAVATIS: I'd go ahead, regardless. I wouldn't leave *my* lovely furniture to rot outside in the rain.

KARAGHIOZIS (*angrily*): Ho! So you'd shove your dirty furniture into my nice clean houses, would you! You'd go scratching my lovely polished floors and knocking chips out of my wonderful carved oak banisters! Well, let me tell you, you big lugworm, that I'd throw all your beastly furniture out of the windows!

HADJIAVATIS (*still more angrily*): What! You slum-scavenger, you'd throw *my* beautiful furniture out of the windows! You'd smash the legs off my Sheraton tables! You'd knock the backs off my Louis XV chairs! You'd crack my old Venetian mirrors! I'll teach you to damage my priceless furniture like that! Come on and I'll eat you at one mouthful!

KARAGHIOZIS (*dancing with rage*): Just try it, you misfaced mandrill! I'll teach you to make free of my magnificent houses without my permission! Come on and I'll tear you in two like an Income Tax Demand!
(*They close and, after a terrific fight, exeunt still struggling.*)

FINIS

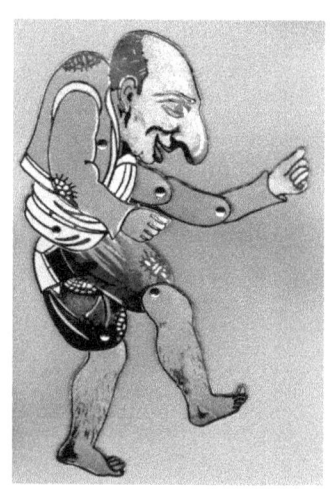

KARAGHIOZIS AND THE ENCHANTED TREE

Barba Yorgos

The Vizier

KARAGHIOZIS AND THE ENCHANTED TREE

PERSONS

KARAGHIOZIS	an engaging and happy-go-lucky hunchback who lives by his wits
HADJIAVATIS	the local town-crier, friend and accomplice of Karaghiozis
KOLLITIRIS	Karaghiozis' small son, a minute replica of his father
THE VIZIER	the local Turkish Governor
TAHIR	the Governor's son
ZAFIRA	Tahir's betrothed
BARBA YORGOS	a mountain shepherd, Karaghiozis' uncle
DERVENAGHAS	the Vizier's Albanian door-keeper
STAVRAKAS	a Piraeus dockside bully, always bragging but backs out of any actual encounter
MEHMET ALI	the local sorcerer

ACT ONE

SCENE ONE

The scene shows THE VIZIER'S *mansion on the right-hand side of the screen, and* KARAGHIOZIS' *dilapidated hut on the left.*

KARAGHIOZIS (*appearing from his hut*): What a world! Nothing but toil or trickery morning, noon and night. And all for what? Just a crust of bread ... and a few other things. Life isn't worth living, as Schopenhauer himself once said to me.

HADJIAVATIS (*entering right and overhearing*): Then why not end it, friend Karaghiozis? Have you ever tried a spot of suicide?

KARAGHIOZIS: I should think I have, Hadjiavatis! But I never seem to manage it somehow. Why, only yesterday I stood for more than an hour with a noose round my neck, and nothing at all happened.

HADJIAVATIS (*laughing*): That's not the way to do it. You shouldn't stand on the ground. You must *suspend* yourself from something.

KARAGHIOZIS: I *did* once. But I felt as if I was choking. I had to cut myself down in a hurry.

HADJIAVATIS: Have you tried shooting yourself?

KARAGHIOZIS: I tried that also. I stole police-sergeant Tsaous' revolver to shoot myself with. But I missed myself with all six shots — although I had the butt actually pressed against my temple!

HADJIAVATIS: That's all wrong, Karaghiozis. Try again with the *barrel* pressed to your temple.

KARAGHIOZIS: Too late now. I sold the revolver and bought half a barrel of wine. Enough to drown my

sorrows, but not myself.
HADJIAVATIS: Then stab yourself to the heart with your knife.
KARAGHIOZIS: Ugh! That would be far too painful — and possibly fatal. Can't you think of a pleasant death; one that I would really enjoy?
HADJIAVATIS: Certainly, Karaghiozis. Why not die the Delightful Death?
KARAGHIOZIS: Ah, that sounds better. Describe it quick; I'm all ears from top to toe!
HADJIAVATIS: Yussuf Ali has just opened a new pastry-cook's shop in the marketplace. Just enter and suicide yourself with a surfeit of Turkish Delight — he has mounds of it. I know that you dote on Turkish Delight; so you couldn't hope for a sweeter death than that!
KARAGHIOZIS (*enthusiastically*): You are a genius, Hadjiavatis! I'll go and commit suicide right away. (*Exit left.*)
HADJIAVATIS (*laughing*): Ha, ha! Friend Karaghiozis doesn't know that Yussuf is Dervenaghas' younger brother, and that Dervenaghas himself is often in the shop. I think we may expect fireworks at any moment! (*Exit right.*)

SCENE TWO

The scene is the same as in Scene One; it is empty. Suddenly a great tumult is heard off-stage on the left, and KARAGHIOZIS *rushes in, hotly pursued by* DERVENAGHAS.

DERVENAGHAS (*knocking* KARAGHIOZIS *down and jumping on him*): Poh yah! Me teach you to eat Turkish Delight! Poh yah! Me teach you to enjoy yourself and not pay!
KARAGHIOZIS (*between yells and groans*): I wasn't enjoying

myself, Dervenaghas, I was committing suicide. But you only gave me time to swallow twenty chunks — not even enough to lose consciousness! And I was quite willing to pay, if you had lent me the money to pay with . . .

DERVENAGHAS (*with one last kick*): Poh yah! You no come no more to die in my brother's shop, or me suicide you good and proper! . . . (*Exit.*)

KARAGHIOZIS (*sitting up and rubbing himself*): What a barbarian! And I know that he's longing for an excuse to suicide me all over again! But I'll spite him by living — no more suicides for me! How was I to know that the shop-owner was Dervenaghas' brother! It was you, Hadjiavatis, who let me in for this! *You* knew all right! But I'll get even with you for your little joke — see if I don't!

(*At that moment* HADJIAVATIS *enters from the left.*)

HADJIAVATIS (*in feigned surprise*): Good gracious, Karaghiozis! What happened to you? You're black and blue all over!

KARAGHIOZIS (*groaning*): It was that brute Dervenaghas. He knocked me down with his motor car!

HADJIAVATIS: But that's impossible! Motor cars haven't been invented yet!

KARAGHIOZIS: Dervenaghas doesn't care a fig for that! And what is more, his Rolls Royce was doing at least 150 miles an hour when it hit me!

HADJIAVATIS: Heavens! A speed like that must surely be illegal on such a congested highway!

KARAGHIOZIS: Of course it is. And Dervenaghas knows it well enough. He even offered me fifty pounds to keep my mouth shut and drop the matter. But I refused. I said I would sue him for one hundred pounds damages.

HADJIAVATIS (*pensively*): Hum, I think you made a mistake there, Karaghiozis. Fifty pounds is a nice little sum. If you go to the law courts to ask for one hundred pounds, it will be the lawyers who will grab the money. You'll be left with just a few pence, or even nothing at all!

KARAGHIOZIS (*pretending to reflect*): You are probably right in what you say, Hadjiavatis, but I'm too bruised to move any distance. I could only crawl to the nearest chemist's shop. Just lend me five pounds for arnica and medical attention, and you run after Dervenaghas and tell him to hand you fifty pounds. Insist upon it. Then deduct your five pounds and another twenty pounds for your trouble.

HADJIAVATIS (*eagerly*): Thank you, friend Karaghiozis, thank you a hundred times. Here are the five pounds, and where will I meet you to give you your share of the money?

KARAGHIOZIS: At the new hospital by the Lycabettus.

HADJIAVATIS: That's too far. I can't walk all that distance.

KARAGHIOZIS: Oh, you won't have to *walk*. You'll be driven there in a comfortable white car — with pretty red crosses painted on it.

HADJIAVATIS: That would be too good to be true, Karaghiozis. But I must hurry. I'll overtake Dervenaghas whom I see over there outside his brother's shop. (*Exit left.*)

KARAGHIOZIS (*gleefully*): Ha, ha, friend Hadjiavatis, here's where I get my own back! You may receive fifty pounds from Dervenaghas, but not the kind of pounds that you're expecting. I must go and see; I think that the disbursement has already started. (*Exit left.*)

(*As* KARAGHIOZIS *goes out, loud howls and the sound of blows are heard off-stage from the direction taken by* HADJIAVATIS.)

ACT TWO

SCENE ONE

The scene is the same as before. KOLLITIRIS *enters right. He goes to* KARAGHIOZIS' *hut and thumps on it with loud shouts.*

KOLLITIRIS: Fadler, fadler, Hadjiavatis told me to tell you to wait for him here. He's got sometling vely importlant to tell you.

KARAGHIOZIS (*appearing from his hut*): Ho, I didn't think old Hadjiavatis would be out of hospital so soon. I wonder what he has to say — it may be something that will put a penny or two in our pockets. (*To* KOLLITIRIS): Thank you, son. I'll give you a lollipop when I manage to steal one.

KOLLITIRIS: But please don't pat me on the head, fadler. I had to steal a big bottle of aspilins the last time you did so. (*Exit.*)

HADJIAVATIS (*entering right*): Ha, there you are, Karaghiozis. It was a dirty trick you played on me last week. But our little jokes must not interfere with business. We can both be of use to each other. Are you willing to go shares, if I put you in the way of earning a hundred pounds? Real pounds cash this time.

KARAGHIOZIS (*ecstatically*): A hundred pounds! Why, of course I'll divide them with you. Just think of all the lamb pilaffes, the egg-plant pies, the fig puddings I could get with fifty pounds! And the tripe and onions, the fish and chips, the sausages and mash — there may even be something left over for Kollitiris' lollipop.

HADJIAVATIS (*insistently*): Do you promise it, Karaghiozis?

KARAGHIOZIS (*importantly*): You have my word.

HADJIAVATIS (*pensively*): I wonder how much your word is worth.

KARAGHIOZIS (*indignantly*): Don't be silly, Hadjiavatis! As town-crier, you have the ears; you know all that's going on in this town. Whilst I have the brains to make use of your information. Thus we both need each other. I'd be a fool to kill the fatted calf — I mean the goose that lays the golden eggs! Unless, of course, someone offered me *two* golden-egg-laying geese. However, the probability statistics are against such an unprecedented eventuality occurring — as Professor Mikelides (who is watching us from the second row) would very elegantly express it.

HADJIAVATIS: True enough, Karaghiozis. The thumb needs the forefinger, and the forefinger needs the thumb to pick a pocket, eh?

KARAGHIOZIS: You've put it in a nutshell, Hadjiavatis. So trot out your news, without any more bushing around the beat. You have all my attention from here to Babel and back!

HADJIAVATIS: Well, the Vizier told me to bring you to him outside his mansion at noon today. He has something of the greatest importance to discuss with you. It is almost twelve now; we had better hurry.

KARAGHIOZIS (*exuberantly*): Right you are. Lead on, MacHadjiavatis!

SCENE TWO

The scene is as before. THE VIZIER *is waiting in front of the door of his mansion.*

THE VIZIER (*grumbling*): I hope they won't keep me waiting too long. Nothing gets on my nerves so much as a

ACT TWO

wait — especially the Christmas variety! Ah, thank goodness, there they are at last!
(KARAGHIOZIS *and* HADJIAVATIS *arrive*.)
HADJIAVATIS (*with a deep bow*): May Your Excellency live for ever!
KARAGHIOZIS (*with a still deeper bow*): May Your Excellency live for more than ever a thousand times over!
THE VIZIER (*to* HADJIAVATIS): Thank you, my good Hadjiavatis, for bringing me Karaghiozis. Here's five pounds for your trouble and now leave us, for what I wish to tell Karaghiozis is strictly private.
HADJIAVATIS (*with more deep bows*): I go, Your Exalted Excellency, I go. And may your shadow never grow less. (*Exit.*)
THE VIZIER (*turning to* KARAGHIOZIS): My son, Tahir, and I are in great distress. You may, perhaps, be able to help us. You will be one hundred pounds the richer if you find a way out of our quandary.
KARAGHIOZIS: I am all eagerness, Your Excellency. The word "pounds" always sets my brains buzzing like a brigade of bluebottles!
THE VIZIER: All the wisest and most virtuous in the land have given up in despair; so I wish to try their opposite for a change. I know, Karaghiozis, that you have the reputation of being the greatest rascal unhung in the whole district; and I now throw the contract into your lap.
KARAGHIOZIS: You flatter me, Your Excellency! And now pray tell me the problem.
THE VIZIER: It is known to all that my dear son, Tahir, was betrothed last month to the beautiful Princess Zafira. Well, she has just been changed into a cow!
KARAGHIOZIS (*in surprise*): A cow! And how do you know she has been changed into a cow?

THE VIZIER: What do you mean, Karaghiozis? Can't I tell the difference between a cow and a lovely girl of seventeen?

KARAGHIOZIS: Seventeen? Ah yes, at that age you can still tell them apart. But what do you wish me to do?

THE VIZIER: I want you to change her back into a girl, of course! But I had better send you to Tahir himself; he will give you the details more clearly than I can. (*Shouting suddenly*): Hola, Dervenaghas, come here!

KARAGHIOZIS (*backing away*): Not Dervenaghas, I beg of you! He and I have a certain incompatibility of temperament.

THE VIZIER: Do not fear, Karaghiozis. I only want him to lead you to my son, Tahir.

DERVENAGHAS (*appearing*): Poh yah, Effendi Vizier. Me thrash Karaghiozis?

THE VIZIER: No, no, Dervenaghas, I only want . . .

DERVENAGHAS (*interrupting*): Poh yah, then me kick him? Me give him little black eye? Me give him little thick ear? . . .

THE VIZIER: No, certainly not. Just conduct him to my son, Tahir Effendi, who is waiting for you both near the blasted oak on the Piraeus-to-Timbuctoo high road.

DERVENAGHAS (*eagerly*): Poh yah, Effendi Vizier, me conduct Karaghiozis with big stick?

THE VIZIER: No, no, I want him to reach my son in one piece.

DERVENAGHAS (*disappointed*): Poh yah, Effendi Vizier, me obey. (*To* KARAGHIOZIS): Come on, you spalpeen,* we go. Me not hurt you *this* time. Me gentle like little bah-lamb.

(DERVENAGHAS *hauls* KARAGHIOZIS *out by the neck.* THE VIZIER *re-enters his mansion.*)

ACT THREE

SCENE ONE

The scene shows a long, flat, empty high road. Near the left-hand edge of the screen there is a leafless blasted oak, with a long branch projecting to the right. TAHIR *is waiting nearby.*

TAHIR (*impatiently*): Ah, here they come. And about time, too! (DERVENAGHAS, *still dragging* KARAGHIOZIS *by the neck, appears from the right.*)

DERVENAGHAS: Poh yah, Effendi Tahir; me conduct Karaghiozis.

KARAGHIOZIS (*indignantly*): Conduct, my foot! You've half throttled me! You'd have ruined my collar, if I'd been wearing one!

TAHIR: Silence, you two. (*To* DERVENAGHAS): You may go now. I wish to talk to Karaghiozis in private. (*To* KARAGHIOZIS): Did my father, the Vizier, tell you what we want you to do?

KARAGHIOZIS (*bowing*): Yes, Your Honour, but I would like a few more details before I undertake so difficult a commission. I only know that Princess Zafira has been transformed into a cow.

TAHIR (*haughtily*): Say "heifer", if you please. It sounds more respectful. I'll call her now; she'll be able to tell you what happened better than I can. (*Calling aloud*): Zafira, Zafira, my love, please come here.
(*A well-endowed cow enters from the right. It has a girl's head bearing two long horns.*)

THE COW (*in a young girl's caressing voice*): Here I am, darling Tahir, what do you want?

TAHIR (*wringing his hands*): Oh, my beloved, when I see you like that, with horns on your dear little head, it breaks my heart in two!

KARAGHIOZIS (*consolingly*): There, there, Tahir Effendi, don't take on so. She's wearing the horns today; you'll be wearing them the day after tomorrow; everything equals out in the end. But may I learn how this incident — I mean catastrophe — occurred?

THE COW (*excitedly*): Oh do manage something for me, Karaghiozis! It's perfectly dreadful to be a cow! I can't get on any of my beautiful silken dresses or yashmaks! My waistline has been absolutely ruined, and my bras simply won't fit across my chest! . . .

KARAGHIOZIS (*interrupting*): No, I'm afraid you'll have to wear them at the udder end. But tell me, Princess, how, when and where did this transformation happen?

THE COW: It happened yesterday afternoon. I don't know how. I just walked under the bough of that blasted oak over there, and the next moment I was a cow!

KARAGHIOZIS (*pensively*): Hum, I wonder, I wonder . . . I have a hypothesis. Now, what does a scientist of note (like Doctor Triphos, there on the right) do when he has a hypothesis? He either chokes on it, or he puts it to the test. Well, I now promote myself to honorary scientist, and I put my hypothesis to the test. I hypothese that the blasted oak over there is mixed up somehow with this affair. But how can I prove it without risking my own valuable hide? (*A harsh voice is heard singing in the distance.*) Ah, here comes Stavrakas, the dockside bully-boy. He's always bragging, but he backs out when it really comes to a fight. I think that he'll do as guinea-pig for Test Number One.

STAVRAKAS (*entering right and bawling lustily*):
They came at me from left and right,

ACT THREE

I faced them and they fled in fright!
They came at me from east and west,
I trounced them till they gave me best!
They came at me from every side
I drew my pistol and they died!
They came at me . . .

KARAGHIOZIS (*interrupting with a slap on the back that nearly knocks* STAVRAKAS *down*): Stop it, Stavrakas, you've half-deafened me!

STAVRAKAS (*menacingly*): Ho, do you mean to provoke me, Karaghiozis? Or did you slap me on the back as a friendly joke?

KARAGHIOZIS: I mean to provoke you, Stavrakas!

STAVRAKAS (*still more menacingly*): Ho, it's lucky for you, Karaghiozis, that you didn't do it for a joke, because I'm a dangerous man to joke with! But be careful that it doesn't happen a second time . . . (KARAGHIOZIS *gives him a stronger slap on the back.*) Or a third time . . . (KARAGHIOZIS *slaps him yet again.*) Or a fourth time . . .

KARAGHIOZIS (*impatiently*): Cut the small talk, Stavrakas. I've known you long enough to know you through and through. But I just wanted to ask you if it's your golden cufflinks which are lying under that tree over there.

STAVRAKAS: Yes, yes, they're the ones I lost yesterday. They fell out of my shirt cuffs as I was twirling my mustachios. Thanks for telling me, Karaghiozis; I'll stand you an *ouzo* when we next meet down by the Piraeus docks.

(STAVRAKAS *rushes under the tree. He promptly disappears underground* and at once reappears in the form of a hare with a man's head and long hare's ears. The hare rushes whimpering to the other end of the screen where it stands as though petrified. There are loud exclamations of surprise from* TAHIR *and*

THE COW.)

KARAGHIOZIS (*triumphantly*): The first test has been a success. We must confirm it scientifically with a second one. Ha, do I hear another guinea-pig approaching!

BARBA YORGOS (*appearing from right and singing lustily*):
Come, come, come,
Come, little donkey,
Come, come, come, come!
Come, come, come,
Come, little donkey, come!

KARAGHIOZIS (*shouting*): Hey, Barba Yorgos, did you leave a large pot of your best yoghourt under that tree over there?

BARBA YORGOS: I don't remember doing so, Nephew Karaghiozis, but I'll go and see.

(*As* BARBA YORGOS *steps beneath the tree, he disappears underground with a loud yell, and reappears as a great shaggy bear with his own human head.* BARBA YORGOS *rushes at* KARAGHIOZIS *with roars of rage.*)

KARAGHIOZIS: Wait, wait, uncle! Don't get excited! You're a successful scientific experiment — a confirmatory test!

BARBA YORGOS (*still more furious*): This is another of your practical jokes, Karaghiozis you rascal! Wait till I catch you — I'll tear your tonsils out!

KARAGHIOZIS (*sheltering behind* TAHIR): Calm yourself, uncle, and let us marshal the facts in a scientific and systematic sequence. Fact number one: Three people have walked under that tree, and each one has been transformed into an animal. Fact number two: To cause such results, that tree must be enchanted. Fact number three: To be enchanted, that tree must have been ensorcered by a sorcerer. Fact number four: Who is the only sorcerer in these parts: Old Mehmet Ali.

Conclusion: That tree was enchanted by Mehmet Ali. Q.E.D.* What must we do now? Fetch Mehmet here, shove him under the tree, and see how he counteracts his own sorcery. Go then Barba Yorgos and do the needful.

(BARBA YORGOS *lumbers out and returns a few minutes later with the wildly struggling* MEHMET ALI *hugged in his embrace.* BARBA YORGOS *pushes* MEHMET *under the tree.* MEHMET *disappears underground, like the others, and instantly reappears as a fat man-headed pig.*)

THE PIG (*triumphantly*): Fools! Don't imagine that you can make me stay like this! See! With one magic word, I will regain my former shape! SOROLOP!

(THE PIG *disappears underground, and at once reappears in his human form.*)

KARAGHIOZIS: Seize him, Tahir Effendi! Don't let him go until everything has been brought to a satisfactory conclusion. (*To the others*): Now then, all you animals, you know what to do. Just say the magic word SOROLOP, and be quick about it!

(*There is a chorus of* SOROLOP, *and the Cow, the Hare, and the Bear all regain their human shapes.* ZAFIRA *falls into* TAHIR'S *eager arms with a cry of joy.* THE VIZIER *enters at that moment, just in time to see the final transformation.*)

THE VIZIER (*sternly to* MEHMET): Disenchant that tree at once. Do not dare to play such tricks again or I shall have you hanged by the neck until you are dead. In future confine yourself to your legitimate official duties of predicting the weather, drawing up horoscopes, and curing warts. You may go, but remember my words. (MEHMET ALI *slinks out, crestfallen.* THE VIZIER *turns to* KARAGHIOZIS.) As for you, Karaghiozis, you have done well. I thank you, and I have great pleasure in handing you the one hundred pounds promised, and another fifty pounds as a token of my approbation. Now retire all of you, and leave me, my dear son, and my beautiful future daughter-in-law, to our recovered happiness. (*Exeunt all.*)

SCENE TWO

The scene shows a grassy meadow with the coping of a well on the left-hand side. KARAGHIOZIS *and* HADJIAVATIS *enter right.* KARAGHIOZIS *is carrying a big packet of banknotes.*

HADJIAVATIS (*gaily*): Here's a nice cool spot, Karaghiozis. Let us sit down and divide the Vizier's one hundred and fifty pounds, as you promised.

KARAGHIOZIS: Isn't that rather a tame ending? Let us dice instead for the money. Winner takes all.

HADJIAVATIS: No thanks, Karaghiozis. I wouldn't dice with you. Your dice are cogged.

KARAGHIOZIS (*indignantly*): Of course my dice are cogged! All the best dice are cogged, like all the best shares are gilt-edged. But I tell you what: I'll only win when the sixes come up; you'll win on *all* the other numbers. Now what do you say to that?

HADJIAVATIS: Thank you, Karaghiozis, thank you. You are a good fellow, and I'll dice with you with pleasure.

KARAGHIOZIS: Well, here we go. And may the best man, myself, win!

(*They both kneel on the grass.* KARAGHIOZIS *places the pile of banknotes on the ground behind him, and the two friends are soon absorbed in their game. At that moment a large goat strolls up and starts eating the banknotes.* HADJIAVATIS *notices first what is happening, just as the goat swallows the last shred of paper.*)

HADJIAVATIS (*in a panic*): Karaghiozis, quick! The goat, the goat!

KARAGHIOZIS (*angrily*): What do you mean by shrieking "The goat, the goat!" You startled me! You made me bite my tongue!

HADJIAVATIS (*furiously*): A horrible goat has just eaten all our hard-earned money! And it's *your* silly fault! Since it was you who put that packet of notes there behind you, you should have kept your eye on it!

KARAGHIOZIS (*still more furiously*): How the hell could I have kept my eye on it — I haven't got an eye in my backside! It's all *your* fault! You should have seen the goat since you were facing it. I've a good mind to give you one on your oversized snout!

HADJIAVATIS (*leaping to his feet*): Try it, you pig-faced pumpkin, and you'll wish that your mother had heard about birth control!

KARAGHIOZIS (*closing with* HADJIAVATIS): Yes, I *will* try it, you misbegotten mandrill! Take that! And that! And that!

(HADJIAVATIS *responds with equal vigour and enthusiasm, and the two locked combatants roll out of sight together. Their yells and the thuds of their elbows die away off-stage in the distance.*)

FINIS

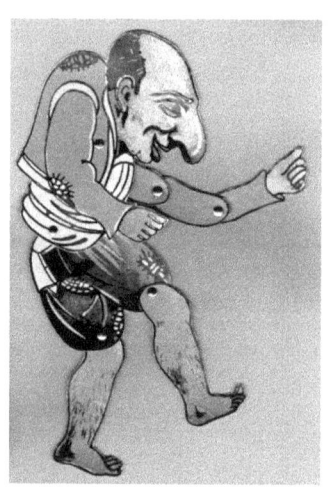

KARAGHIOZIS, ALEXANDER THE GREAT, AND THE DREADFUL DRAGON

KARAGHIOZIS, ALEXANDER THE GREAT, AND THE DREADFUL DRAGON

PERSONS

KARAGHIOZIS	an engaging and happy-go-lucky hunchback who lives by his wits
HADJIAVATIS	the local town-crier, friend and accomplice of Karaghiozis
THE PASHA	a high Turkish official
TAHIR BEY	the Pasha's son
PRINCESS FATIMAH	the Pasha's daughter
SIOR NIONIOS	an impoverished Zantiote aristocrat
MORPHONIOS	the Governor's son
STAVRAKAS	a Piraeus dock-side tough, always bragging but backs out of any actual encounter
DERVENAGHAS	the Vizier's Albanian door-keeper
BARBA YORGOS	a mountain shepherd, Karaghiozis' uncle
ALEXANDER THE GREAT	a tall warrior who appears in full Ancient Greek panoply — crested helmet, sword, spear and shield
THE DREADFUL DRAGON	a many-jointed monster, with huge head, sharp-toothed jaws and a barbed tail

Set in a mixture of Past and Present

ACT ONE

SCENE ONE

The scene shows the Pasha's palace on the right-hand side of the screen, and KARAGHIOZIS' *tumbledown hut on the left.*

HADJIAVATIS (*entering left, singing*):
 I raise my voice and say my piece,
 The people flock and listen:
 A necklace lost, a rich reward —
 Their eyes grow big and glisten . . .
 But tell them of a tax to pay,
 And watch the whole crowd melt away!
 Lelila, oyez! . . . Lelilo, oyez!

TAHIR BEY (*entering right, also singing*):
 I saw a bird upon a tree,
 Upon a mountain pine;
 It sang and mourned its absent love,
 As I too yearn for mine.
 I said to it . . .
 (*breaks off as* HADJIAVATIS *approaches, and shouts to him*): Hi there, Hadjiavatis! You're just the man I was looking for! My father, the Pasha, wants to speak to you in his palace. Urgent! It's about the Dreadful Dragon that's devastating the whole countryside!

HADJIAVATIS (*in surprise*): Dragon? . . . What Dragon? . . .

TAHIR BEY: Where *have* you been this last week, Hadjiavatis? *The* Dragon! Haven't you heard of the flaming Dragon that has been committing arson all over the place, and devouring whole populations after roasting them like popcorn!

HADJIAVATIS: Yes, Your Honour, I *did* hear vague

rumours of unusual occurrences somewhere-or-other. But I just took them for tall tales told in taverns by tittupping topers.

TAHIR BEY: Well, my good man, I hope that you won't bump into *this* particular tall tale. The results might be fatal! But don't waste any more time. My father wishes to make use of your services as official town-crier. Go into the palace and learn the details for yourself.

HADJIAVATIS (*bowing low*): I go, Your Honour, I go.

(HADJIAVATIS *enters the palace;* TAHIR BEY *exit left.*)

SCENE TWO

The scene is the same as in Scene One.

HADJIAVATIS (*entering left, speaking to himself*): Well, that was a pleasant interview with the Pasha. And lucrative too. He'll give me five pounds to cry his proclamation all over the north side of the town. And he asked me to engage a deputy town-crier, for another five pounds, to do the same in the south. Just the job for my good friend, Karaghiozis. Ah, here we are at the Karaghiozis Mansion . . . I'll call him. (*He thumps on the hut door and shouts*): Karaghiozis, hi Karaghiozis, come out!

KARAGHIOZIS (*from within*): Stop that row, you idiot! I was dreaming that I was in the Claridge's grill-room. The head-waiter had brought me a huge silver bowl of bean soup and pig's trotters. I was just about to eat, when you went and woke me! Get out! I want to go back to sleep before they take the bowl away! Beat it, you damned dream-dissipater!

HADJIAVATIS: Forget your silly dream, Karaghiozis. I have something to tell you that will put five pounds in your

ACT ONE

pocket.

KARAGHIOZIS (*emerging from his hut with a rush*): Ah, that's different, Hadjiavatis. Tell me quick!

HADJIAVATIS: The Pasha wants us to cry his proclamation through the town. I in the north and you in the south. We will each get five pounds for our trouble.

KARAGHIOZIS: I'm willing, Hadjiavatis. But I've never town-cried before. What must I say, and how must I say it?

HADJIAVATIS: It's quite easy, my friend. Watch me now and listen. Then do exactly like me. (*He shouts in a loud, shrill voice*): Oyez! Oyez! Hear me, O people all. Take heed, O Americans, Britons, Copts, Danes, Ecuadorians, Frenchmen, Germans, Hollanders, Italians, Jamaicans, Kalmuks, Lithuanians . . .

KARAGHIOZIS (*interrupting impatiently*): Yes, yes, let's skip the rest of the ethnography . . . what is the *message?*

HADJIAVATIS: Er . . . I've clean forgotten! . . . It's all your fault, Karaghiozis, you flustered me! Wait, let me think. (*After a long pause*): Oh, ah, yes . . . I remember now. We must both cry: "His Highness the Pasha decrees thus: He who slays the Dreadful Dragon that is devastating the countryside, and brings its head to the Pasha, will receive a reward of a thousand pounds and the hand in marriage of beautiful Princess Fatimah, the Pasha's daughter." There now, Karaghiozis, can you repeat all that?

KARAGHIOZIS (*confidently*): Of course I can, Hadjiavatis. Just listen. (*He shouts in a deep, rumbling base*): Oyez! Oyez! Hear me, O steeples all. Take heed, O Asparagusians, Beefsteakians, Carrotians, Dumplingians, Endivians, Fishandchipians . . .

HADJIAVATIS (*interrupting*): Stop, that won't do, Karaghiozis! Can't you think of anything else except about eating and eatables?

KARAGHIOZIS: What else *is* there to think about?

HADJIAVATIS: And anyway, your voice is all wrong. You must pitch it a good deal higher.

KARAGHIOZIS: Higher? Well, that's easy, Hadjiavatis. Just wait a minute. (*He goes out and returns with a stepladder, which he climbs.*) Ought I to pitch my voice as high as the top of this ladder, or will half-way do?

HADJIAVATIS: Don't be silly, Karaghiozis. It's only your *voice* that should be higher, the rest of you must stay on the ground. And now can you repeat the important part of the Pasha's proclamation?

KARAGHIOZIS: Of course I can. Just listen (*he declaims in a shrill falsetto voice*): He who slays the Pasha who is devastating the Dreadful Dragon . . . No, no, I mean: He who has knives to grind and scissors to mend and brings them to the Pasha . . . No, no I mean . . . But, Hadjiavatis, a brilliant idea has just struck me! . . .

HADJIAVATIS: And what is this marvellous idea of yours?

KARAGHIOZIS (*enthusiastically*): Why should we be fobbed off with a miserable five pounds each for all our toil and trouble in crying the Pasha's proclamation? Let us both go and kill the Dreadful Dragon ourselves, and then we can divide the thousand pounds and the Princess between us!

HADJIAVATIS: Hum . . . Have you *seen* the Dreadful Dragon?

KARAGHIOZIS: Yes, I have.

HADJIAVATIS: And at what distance?

KARAGHIOZIS: About a mile and a half. I had a good look at it through the Hodja's* telescope.

HADJIAVATIS: You had a *good* look at it, you say?

KARAGHIOZIS: Yes, and terrible it was I can tell you! The

ACT ONE

telescope showed it as plain as plain! It made my hair stand on end!

HADJIAVATIS: It made your hair stand on end! And yet you knew that the Dreadful Dragon was a good mile and a half away. Have you reflected that to cut off its head you would have to approach within a *yard* of it?

KARAGHIOZIS (*after a long pause*): Oh, ah, I get what you mean ... Oh well, five pounds is quite a nice little sum. One can buy a whole lot of bean soup and fish and chips for five pounds.

HADJIAVATIS: So one can, Karaghiozis. But let us be on our way. And I'd better give you a little more tutoring in the noble art of town-crying as we go along.

(*They both exit left.*)

ACT TWO

SCENE ONE

The scene shows an open plain. To the left one sees the distant houses of the town, and to the right a rocky hillock where the Dreadful Dragon has its lair. KARAGHIOZIS *and* HADJIAVATIS *enter left.*

KARAGHIOZIS (*mopping his brow*): Well, Hadjiavatis, I think that was a job jolly well done. The whole town knows now about the Pasha's reward for killing the Dreadful Dragon. I wonder who'll be the first fool to try his luck. (*A voice is heard off-stage to the left, singing.*) Ah, here comes the first candidate for dragonian digestion. And bless me if it isn't our old friend Sior Nionios, the Pride of Zante.

(SIOR NIONIOS *enters left*)

SIOR NIONIOS (*singing*):
  I plucked my love a snow-white rose;
  She kissed it — and I said:
  Oh love, from envy of your lips
  That rose now blushes red!
  Ah, Zante, Zante, by the sea,
  I would that I were there;
  Its houses are as tall can be,
  Its maidens ever fair!
  Ha tra-la-la! Ha tra-la-lo!
  Ha tra-la-lee . . .

(*breaks off on seeing the other two*) Ah, Karaghiozis, is this the way to the Dreadful Dragon's den? I wish to be the first to kill it and earn the Pasha's reward. With one thrust of my trusty stiletto I'll pin it to the ground; and then with a quick slash I'll cut off its head! No Monster can escape *me*, Sior Nionios! Where is that Dreadful

Dragon? Let me get at him!

(*A terrific roar is heard from behind the hillock.*)

SIOR NIONIOS (*in a somewhat smaller voice*): Er... er... was *that* the Dreadful Dragon?

HADJIAVATIS: That was the Dragon all right. It seems to be in one of its milder moods today.

KARAGHIOZIS: Yes, you're lucky, Sior Nionios. The Dreadful Dragon is probably digesting that lion it demolished a few hours ago. Just dash in whilst it is still somnolent and cut off its head. (*There is another still louder bellow from the hillock.*) Quick now to the attack! Forwards, brave heart!

SIOR NIONIOS: Er... ah... yes... Forwards, brave heart — but backwards, swift feet!

(*He exits hurriedly by the way he came.*)

KARAGHIOZIS: Well, Hadjiavatis, I suppose we can count that as a win for the Dreadful Dragon. Sior Nionios seemed actually to be afraid of it! Can you imagine such pusillamo... such pusillami... mi... mity! He should have rushed in and slain with one swift, slashing stiletto sweep. That's what *I* would have done!

HADJIAVATIS: Nobody's preventing you, Karaghiozis. Rush in and start swift, slashing stiletto-sweeping!

KARAGHIOZIS: Unfortunately, I can't, Hadjiavatis. I sprained my wrist yesterday whilst playing chess. And, anyway, I haven't got a stiletto. But hark! I hear someone approaching. I think I recognise Stavrakas' voice.

HADJIAVATIS: No mistaking *that* croak! Here comes candidate number two.

STAVRAKAS (*entering left and singing in a discordant voice; he has a pistol almost as big as himself stuck in his waistband*):

They all attacked me in a bunch,
I killed the lot before my lunch!

They charged again — I did not flee;
I killed a score and then had tea!
Once more they . . .
(*breaks off as he draws near*) Hullo, Karaghiozis! Hullo, Hadjiavatis! I hope I'm not too late to kill the Dreadful Dragon. I had to slink here by the back-streets, or the police might have arrested me for carrying a concealed weapon. Has anyone forestalled me?

KARAGHIOZIS: No, Stavrakas, nobody has forestalled you. You can walk straight into the Dreadful Dragon's parlour. But I hope that you have made your will and left all your estate in good order.

STAVRAKAS: Nonsense, Karaghiozis. I'll eat that Dreadful Dragon at a single mouthful. Just wait until you hear the bang of my trusty *koumboura*.* I'll win the thousand pounds and the Princess before you can even wink!
(*Exits right towards the Dragon's lair.*)

KARAGHIOZIS: There, Hadjiavatis, there goes that windbag. I hope the Dreadful Dragon makes a meal of him. Piraeus will be a purer, paradisiacal place.
(*A bang is heard off-stage; then a yell from* STAVRAKAS, *choking and retching, and* STAVRAKAS *is suddenly hurled head-over-heels across the stage and vanishes left with a howl.*)

HADJIAVATIS: Even a Dragon's stomach could not stand that swine of a Stavrakas! It spewed him out like a peck of pickled poison!

KARAGHIOZIS: Aye, more's the pity! There'll be some mourning in Piraeus when the news gets round that Stavrakas is still in our midst. And now, here comes the third candidate.
(*A grating, nasal voice is heard off-stage, left.*)

MORPHONIOS (*entering, singing*):
There's none like me in all the world

So handsome and so graceful;
One look at me, and every maid
Finds other men distasteful!
I break their hearts as I go by,
I hear them moan, I hear them sigh,
But I walk on with nose in air,
And leave them all bewailing there,
And never . . .
(MORPHONIOS *breaks off as* KARAGHIOZIS *gives him a hefty slap on the back.*)

KARAGHIOZIS: So you're off, I see, to kill the Dreadful Dragon, Morphonios my boy!

MORPHONIOS (*haughtily*): No, I'm not. I *had* intended to kill it and win the Princess for my bride, but the Pasha has given strict orders that I must on no account make the attempt. He threatens to imprison me in a deep, dark, dank dungeon, if I should approach within fifty yards of the Dreadful Dragon's damp, dismal den. He holds my life to be far too precious to risk. (*Walks away with a mincing step and exits right.*)

HADJIAVATIS: My goodness! What do you make of that, Karaghiozis? Why the Pasha's sudden concern for the life of that obnoxious object?

KARAGHIOZIS: The answer is easy, Hadjiavatis. Our wise Pasha knows that Dame Fortune delights in fabulous flukes. Morphonios *might* kill the Monster. It *might* drop dead just at the sight of him! And the Pasha would rather have the Dreadful Dragon than a Dreadful Son-in-law like Morphonios. Q.E.D., as my old Nanny used to say.

HADJIAVATIS: I think you're right there, Karaghiozis. The Dreadful Dragon would certainly be the lesser of two evils. But hist! Here comes another candidate.

SCENE TWO

The scene is the same as in Scene One.
DERVENAGHAS (*entering, singing*):
   Poh yah, me pat the Dragon's head,
   Poh yah, the Dragon he fall dead!
   Me win the Princess, pat her head,
   But gently so she no fall dead!
   Poh yah . . .
   (DERVENAGHAS *sees* KARAGHIOZIS. *He breaks off his song, and promptly knocks* KARAGHIOZIS *down.*)
KARAGHIOZIS (*getting up and rubbing himself*): Hey, Dervenaghas, why did you do that? I was not annoying you in any way! Why are you angry with me?
DERVENAGHAS: Poh yah, me no angry. Me only practising for fight with Dreadful Dragon. Poh yah, me just tuning up. Me unlimbering muscle.
   (DERVENAGHAS *knocks* KARAGHIOZIS *down a second time, and also knocks* HADJIAVATIS *down for good measure. He then stalks out right.*)
KARAGHIOZIS (*to* HADJIAVATIS, *as they both rub themselves*): The brute! I hope that the Dreadful Dragon will savour him slowly. With plenty of oil and vinegar.
   (*At that moment* DERVENAGHAS *reappears hurriedly from right.*)
KARAGHIOZIS: You've killed the Dreadful Dragon very quickly, Dervenaghas! And now, I suppose, you're off to embrace the thousand pounds and the beautiful Princess!
DERVENAGHAS: Poh yah, me no kill Dreadful Dragon *yet*. Him too big. No can reach to pat on head. Me practise more. Poh yah, *then* me kill!
   (DERVENAGHAS *knocks down* KARAGHIOZIS *and* HAD-

JIAVATIS *once again, and strides out, left.*)
KARAGHIOZIS (*picking himself up and rubbing himself as before*):
Oh, the barbarian! He would have ruined my collar had I been wearing one! I hope he practises himself to death! But here comes still another candidate.
BARBA YORGOS (*entering left, singing*):
I loved a maiden fair, and how!
She was as dainty as a cow,
And in her eyes so soft and brown,
I gazed until the sun went down.
Be mine, I beg you on my knees,
Be mine, sweet maid, I'll bring you cheese,
I'll bring you milk, I'll bring you fruit,
I'll feed you on my best yoghourt.
Be mine, be mine . . .
(*breaks off on seeing* KARAGHIOZIS) Hullo, is that you, Nephew Karaghiozis!
KARAGHIOZIS (*hurriedly*): No, no, Uncle, *please* don't pat me on the head. I've been pummelled enough already by that brute of a Dervenaghas! But are *you* also off to kill the Dreadful Dragon?
BARBA YORGOS: And why not, Nephew Karaghiozis? A thousand pounds is a nice round sum. Not counting the Princess — though I don't know what my Old Woman will have to say about that!
KARAGHIOZIS: You may be sure that Auntie will have *plenty* to say about that, my dear Uncle!
BARBA YORGOS: That's just what I'm afraid of, Nephew. But we'll cross that bridge when we come to it. In the meanwhile I must slaughter the Dreadful Dragon. Let me get my crook round its neck, and I'll flatten it like a pat of fresh butter!
(BARBA YORGOS *moves behind the hillock, right. There is the*

noise of a terrific battle. Sometimes BARBA YORGOS' *head is seen above the hillock, sometimes the Dragon's. A barbed tail waves to and fro. Suddenly there is the sound of a tremendous sneeze, and* BARBA YORGOS *is blown head-over-heels to the centre of the stage.*)

BARBA YORGOS (*picking himself up and rubbing himself*): Aie, the saints preserve us! That Dreadful Dragon was bigger than my biggest bull. It nearly got me! I'd have been dead as a pork sausage by now, if the Monster hadn't crushed the snuff-box in my belt-pouch and sniffed up a good snout full!

KARAGHIOZIS: But won't you go back to kill the Dreadful Dragon, Uncle?

BARBA YORGOS (*emphatically*): No, Nephew Karaghiozis, I will not! Enough is as good as a feast. The Dreadful Dragon got my crook, but it didn't get *me!* And there is a another blessing too: I won't have to explain the Princess to my Old Woman. That at least is something for which to praise the saints! (*Exits left.*)

ACT THREE

SCENE ONE

The scene is the same as the last in Act Two, except that the hillock to the right, where the Monster has its lair, is shown nearer and larger. KARAGHIOZIS *is standing to the left of the screen.*

KARAGHIOZIS (*to himself*): No other candidate has appeared since Barba Yorgos threw up the contract yesterday. It looks as if the Dreadful Dragon will devastate us all at its leisure . . . to slow music . . . Hullo, what's happening? . . . What's this? . . . Who are you? . . .

(*There is a sudden flash of red fire, and a tall warrior appears before* KARAGHIOZIS. *He wears a complete Ancient Greek panoply, with sword, spear, shield, and a high crested helmet.*)

THE WARRIOR (*in a ringing voice*): Hail to thee! I am Alexander the Great in person!

KARAGHIOZIS (*amazed, but unabashed*): You can't be! Alexander the Great died of a fever at least 200 years ago!

ALEXANDER: Aye, I died, alas! In bed instead of on the battlefield as I would have preferred. Charon* defeated me by an underhand trick and dragged me down to Hades.

KARAGHIOZIS: Then why aren't you in Hades still?

ALEXANDER (*in high-flown, pedantic Greek**): Charon still feared me. He trembled lest I should launch a putsch and wrest his kingdom from his grasp; and so he banished me from his realm. I belong now neither to the World Above nor to the World Below. I roam Earth and Sky at my will, and I pass my time in righting wrongs and slaying foul Monsters. That is why I am here. I intend to kill yon villainous Dragon and deliver this countryside from its dark nightmare. 'Twill be an easy task. (ALEXANDER *stalks towards the hillock, and calls loudly*): Come hither, thou baleful Monster!

KARAGHIOZIS (*striking a heroic pose, and trying to imitate* ALEXANDER'S *language — most of which he has not understood*): Aye, come hither, thou pailful Songster! And if thou comest not hither, I'll come and hither thee myself!

(*There is no sign from the Dragon's lair; no Monster appears.*)

ALEXANDER: The Dreadful Dragon has sensed its peril. It knows that I, Alexander, am on its trail; and it has retreated to the depths of its den where I cannot reach it. And here, O friend Karaghiozis, thou canst aid me in my task.

KARAGHIOZIS: How canst I aid thee, O mighty Monarch?

ALEXANDER: Thou canst go and tempt the Dreadful Dragon out by acting as decoy-duck.

KARAGHIOZIS: Aye, and how canst I best act thus, O great Alexander?

ALEXANDER: Thy role will be an easy one, O Karaghiozis. Thou must stand at the mouth of the Dreadful Dragon's den and make faces at it. In its rage, it will issue forth to wreak vengeance on thee. That will afford me an opportunity of dealing it its quietus.

KARAGHIOZIS (*dubiously*): But what if the Monster lashes at me with its barbed tail whilst I am acting as decoy-duck?

ALEXANDER: Then thou must duck, O Karaghiozis! But fear not; I will be there. And if by mischance thou art slain, I will assume full responsibility. I assure thee that thy dependants shall receive most generous compensation.

KARAGHIOZIS (*still more dubiously*): That would indeed be a great consolation! But couldn't I act as decoy-duck through a telescope? The Hodja has a good long-distance one that I could borrow ...
(*At that moment the Dreadful Dragon dashes out, roaring, from its lair.* KARAGHIOZIS *retreats prudently to the extreme left corner of the stage.* ALEXANDER *attacks the Monster and, after a terrific fight, kills it.*)
KARAGHIOZIS (*returning to the middle of stage*): Hurrah, we've done it! We've killed the Dreadful Dragon! Thanks to my expert decoy-ducking — helped, of course, by thee with thy sword and spear.
ALEXANDER (*amused*): Put it that way if thou likest, my good friend. *We* killed the Dreadful Dragon; and then *we* cut off its head with *our* sword! But before conveying it to the Pasha, I will betake myself to yon lakelet and cleanse myself from the blood and sweat of battle.
(ALEXANDER *exits right, leaving the Dragon's severed head in the middle of the stage.*)

SCENE TWO

The scene is the same as before, except that a closer view of the Dragon's severed head is shown. It now occupies most of the centre of the stage. KARAGHIOZIS *approaches it cautiously.*
KARAGHIOZIS (*to himself*): Good gracious! What an enormous head — and what huge jaws and teeth! It was certainly courageous of me to act as decoy-duck. It was solely due to my heroic decoy-ducking that the Dreadful Dragon got its deserts! Then why not take its head to the Pasha and claim the just reward to which I am morally entitled! In fact it would be insulting Providence if I did *not*

do so! Come then with me, my beauty! (*Tries to lift the huge head and finds that he can't even budge it*): Hum, what do I do now? Ha, I've got it! I'll just cut out the tongue and take that. The Pasha will know that the Dreadful Dragon must be really and truly dead, for it to allow me to hack off such a vital organ. So here goes!

(*With a good deal of effort and swearing,* KARAGHIOZIS *manages to prop open the Dragon's ponderous jaws and cut out the enormous tongue. It is almost more than* KARAGHIOZIS *can carry, and he totters off the stage, left, with it on his back.*)

ACT FOUR

SCENE ONE

The scene is the same as in Scene One of Act One. THE PASHA *is standing in front of the door of his palace, talking to his son,* TAHIR BEY.

THE PASHA (*gloomily*): There does not seem to have been any enthusiastic response to my proclamation. I hear that only Sior Nionios, Stavrakas,* my factotum Dervenaghas, and that boorish shepherd Barba Yorgos have volunteered so far. And they all have only just escaped with their lives! It looks as if I shall be saddled with that Dreadful Dragon for the rest of my natural existence. And the Sultan, may his shadow never grow less, will be itching to cut that existence short if this province is further ruined and more valuable tax-payers liquidated. Aye, my son, I can already imagine him twiddling his bow-string!*

TAHIR BEY: Have courage, father. I can hear someone approaching... he may be the bearer of good news.
(*There is the sound of much puffing and blowing, and* KARAGHIOZIS *staggers in, left, bent double under the weight of the Dragon's huge tongue.*)

KARAGHIOZIS (*triumphantly, as he casts the tongue at the feet of* THE PASHA): There, Your Honour, there is the Dreadful Dragon's tongue — proof that the Monster is indeed dead! I claim the promised reward. Let the betrothal feast be for tonight and the wedding tomorrow morning.

THE PASHA (*without much elation*): My word is my bond. All shall be done as you wish, my brave Karaghiozis. Depart now and return to my palace one hour after sunset. The feast and the bride-to-be will be ready.

KARAGHIOZIS (*loftily*): Oh, and don't forget to invite my good friend, Hadjiavatis. He will be chief guest at the feast and best-man at the wedding tomorrow.

THE PASHA: That will be attended to also, O noble Karaghiozis.

(KARAGHIOZIS *exits left.* THE PASHA *and* TAHIR BEY *enter the palace.*)

SCENE TWO

The scene shows a sumptuous room inside THE PASHA'S *palace.* THE PASHA *and his daughter,* PRINCESS FATIMAH, *enter right and left.*

PRINCESS FATIMAH (*furiously*): A nice thing you have let me in for, father! Fancy having to marry that good-for-nothing rascal, Karaghiozis! Can't you cancel the whole affair?

THE PASHA (*gravely*): I'm afraid not, my daughter. My word is my bond. I could scarcely break it after so many ears have heard my proclamation. It would create a most unfortunate impression. But cheer up, my darling. Life is fleeting and uncertain in this vale of tears — as many philosophers, much wiser than myself, have pointed out. I have a presentiment that Karaghiozis will meet with a fatal accident in the very near future. He may, for instance, slip on a banana-skin and fall, just by chance, against Dervenaghas' yataghan.* Have courage, my sweet daughter, I predict that you will be a merry widow before the month is ended.

SCENE THREE

The scene depicts a part of THE PASHA'S *park. Many small trees and rosebushes are seen, together with a distant view of the palace at left. From off-stage, right, comes the sound of music and the hubbub of a well-attended feast.* KARAGHIOZIS' *voice is heard above the din, shouting loudly.*

KARAGHIOZIS (*off-stage*): Hey, waiter, bring me some more caviar. And serve it with a spade, not with a salt-spoon! And, waiter, refill my glass and that of my good friend Hadjiavatis with champagne. Or, better still, leave us the whole bottle!

HADJIAVATIS (*off-stage*): The Pasha is certainly doing us proud, friend Karaghiozis! I never knew that there was so much food to eat in the whole world! My cummerbund will split in another minute!

KARAGHIOZIS (*off-stage*): Hey, waiter, bring me another helping of lamb-pilaffe. And heap it on with a shovel!
(*The noise of the feast still continues off-stage, as* THE PASHA *and* TAHIR BEY *appear on the screen, right.*)

THE PASHA: Well, Tahir, everyone seems to be enjoying a good guzzle at my expense. I simply can't imagine how those two scamps, Karaghiozis and Hadjiavatis, can put so much food away! They must be built hollow inside.

TAHIR BEY: They must indeed, father! But hark! What is that sound I hear?
(*The tramp of heavy footsteps is heard off-stage, left, and* ALEXANDER THE GREAT *enters, bearing on his shoulders the huge head of the Dragon. He casts it down with a crash in front of* THE PASHA.)

ALEXANDER: There, O Pasha, there is the Dreadful Dragon's head. The Monster fell beneath my sword and spear!

THE PASHA (*in surprise*): But Karaghiozis has claimed that

he killed the Dreadful Dragon! This matter must be looked into at once. Ho, Dervenaghas, fetch Karaghiozis here with the utmost immediacy and forthwithness!

DERVENAGHAS (*off-stage, right*): Poh yah, Effendi Pasha. Me fetch him pronto!

KARAGHIOZIS (*off-stage, right*): Lemme go, you gorilla! You're crumpling my shirtfront! You're spilling my coffee all down my waistcoat! You're choking me on my caviar sandwich!

(*The next moment* DERVENAGHAS *enters right, dragging a protesting* KARAGHIOZIS *by the neck.*)

ALEXANDER (*much amused*): Ah-ha, my friend Karaghiozis! So thou didst cut out the Dragon's tongue — to pretend that *thou* hadst killed it with thy little hatchet, eh?

KARAGHIOZIS (*indignantly*): No, no, Your Majesty, you've got it all wrong! I cut out the tongue to make the Dragon's huge head lighter for you to carry here. I did it for your sake — to save you from a possible inguinal* rupture.

THE PASHA (*furiously*): But you told me that *you* had killed the Dreadful Dragon. You claimed the reward, and even clamoured for the betrothal feast to take place today and the wedding tomorrow!

KARAGHIOZIS (*deprecatingly*): No, no, Your Honour; you too have got me all wrong! I simply said that the Dreadful Dragon was dead — I did not say that *I* had killed it. And I claimed the promised reward not for myself, but for my good master, Alexander, here. I knew that he would turn up at any moment, and that is why I suggested that the betrothal feast and the wedding should take place as soon as possible. It was on *his* behalf that I was organising everything.

ACT FOUR

ALEXANDER (*laughing*): Thou sly rogue! And it was for *my* sake, no doubt, that thou didst stuff thyself on caviar, lamb-pilaffe, and champagne!

KARAGHIOZIS (*humbly*): Forgive me, Your Majesty. I had to while away the time somehow, whilst awaiting your somewhat delayed arrival.

THE PASHA (*to* ALEXANDER): Then it is to Your Majesty, and not to this wretch of a Karaghiozis, that I owe the promised reward!

ALEXANDER: Thou owest me nothing, my dear Pasha. I only seek for honour and glory, and the chance of doing a good deed, as I roam the Upper World. Fate does not allow me to tarry long in any place. Give the reward to Karaghiozis if thou wishest; I resign all my rights in his favour. And now I must depart. May good fortune ever smile upon you all. (*Exits right in a flash of red light.*)

KARAGHIOZIS (*dancing a happy jig*): Hurrah! Hurrah! You heard what he said, Your Honour! He resigns all his rights in my favour! So on with the feast! Let joy be unrefined!

THE PASHA (*ominously*): Yes, Karaghiozis, I heard what he said. You shall have your rights — you shall be paid in full! (*Shouting to* DERVENAGHAS): Hola, Dervenaghas, conduct Sir Karaghiozis off the premises and give him as many rights as he can digest! And you can throw in some lefts as well!

DERVENAGHAS (*gleefully*): Poh yah, Effendi Pasha! Me conduct Karaghiozis good and proper!

(DERVENAGHAS *hauls* KARAGHIOZIS *out by the neck, left. The sound of blows and howls is heard dying away in the distance.*)

SCENE FOUR

The scene shows an open field; KARAGHIOZIS' *hut is seen in the background, left.* KARAGHIOZIS *and* HADJIAVATIS *enter from opposite sides of the screen.*

HADJIAVATIS: You should have warned me, friend Karaghiozis. When that animal of a Dervenaghas had finished with you, he came and threw *me* out also! My ribs are still black and blue!

KARAGHIOZIS: And so are mine, Hadjiavatis. But the heavenly gorge we had was well worth it! You must admit that we never stuffed so much in our whole lives! And, as a bonus, I did not have to break any news about marrying Princesses to *my* Old Woman. So the sun still shines and all's fairly right with the world!

HADJIAVATIS: Now let us finish our little business, and then to bed.

KARAGHIOZIS: What little business are you talking about, Hadjiavatis?

HADJIAVATIS: Why, the fight with which we end the last act of every shadow-show entertainment. Our devoted audience expects it of us. The lights can't go out until we roll off the screen, locked in a terrific, titanic tussle!

KARAGHIOZIS: You're right, Hadjiavatis, I had quite forgotten it. Well, what shall we quarrel about *this* time?

HADJIAVATIS: Anything you like, Karaghiozis, so long as it is sufficiently inconsequential. For instance, would you say that the moon was made of green cheese?

KARAGHIOZIS: No, certainly not, Hadjiavatis.

HADJIAVATIS: Well, I say it *is*, you pig-faced baboon!

KARAGHIOZIS: It *isn't*, you flea-infested jackass!

(They close with imprecations and insults and roll, fighting madly,

ACT FOUR

off the screen, left. Their yells and the thud of their blows fade off-stage in the distance.)

FINIS

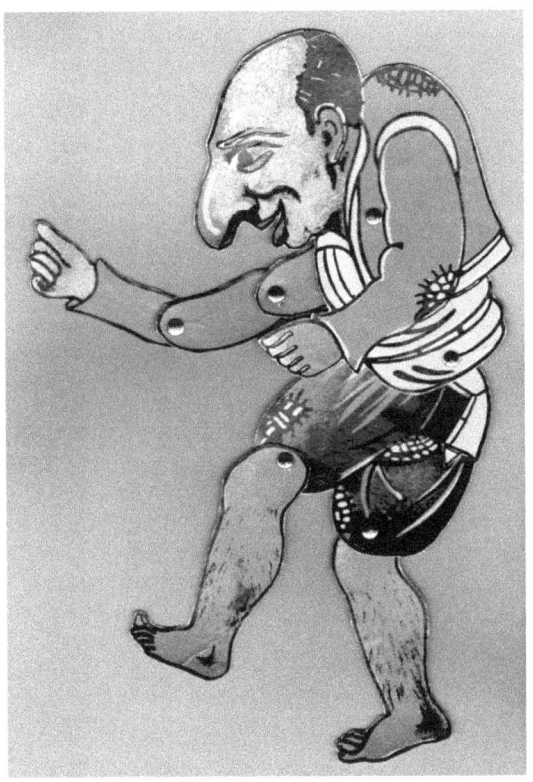

NOTES

[TS] identifies Theodore Stephanides' original notes.
[Eds] identifies notes or parts of notes added by the editors.

18. Zantiote. A person from Zante (the Italian name for the Ionian island of Zakynthos) [Eds].

21. Xylophagy. "Wood-eating", that is, being beaten by a stick or wooden implement; from Ancient Greek *xylon* ("wood") and *phagein* ("to consume *or* eat"). The Modern Greek for "eat wood" is commonly used to mean "get a beating". The words "Xylophagy" and "Xylophobia" (used on pages 13 and 23, and explained on page 13 as "an inordinate fear of wood") were probably coined by Stephanides [Eds].

28. L.S.D. Pronounced as shown (three separate letters) but usually printed as "£.s.d.", referring to the pounds, shillings and pence of UK pre-decimal currency (12 pence = 1 shilling; 20 shillings = 1 pound). The letters actually denote the Latin names of Roman units: *librae*, *solidi* and *denarii* [Eds].

29. selimitis. *Selimiasmos* in the original Greek. A play on the name Selim and the word *seliniasmos* i.e. epilepsy [TS]. *Selinisiasmos* derives from *selini*, the Greek for "moon", reflecting the belief that epileptic seizures were influenced by the moon. Compare the English term "moonstruck" [Eds].

33. the *Queen Mary*. Karaghiozis would, of course, use a more up-to-date simile today [TS]. RMS *Queen Mary*, a Cunard Line ocean liner, was the second-largest passenger ship in the world at the time of her launch in 1936. In use until 1967, mainly for Atlantic crossings, the *Queen Mary* is now permanently moored as a tourist attraction at Long Beach, California [Eds].

35. Effendi. Title of respect or courtesy. It should follow the name or title of the person addressed, but Devernaghas always says, incorrectly, "Effendi Vizier" and so on. [Eds].

52. spalpeen. From Irish *spailpín* (with stress on the second syllable), meaning an itinerant seasonal labourer; in English it came to mean "rascal" or "layabout".

55. *He promptly disappears underground.* The puppeteer is obliged to dip the puppet below the level of the screen, to be able to substitute the appropriate one showing the metamorphosis [TS].

57. Q.E.D. *Quod erat demonstrandum*: "what was to be demonstrated". The letters Q.E.D. are often placed at the end of a successful mathematical proof or logical argument [Eds].

66. Hodja. A Muslim schoolmaster [Eds].

70. *Koumboura.* A kind of large pistol much favoured by Piraeus dockside swashbucklers [TS].

75. Charon. In Medieval and Modern Greek folklore, Charon has become the *Black Horseman*, the personification of Death himself [TS]. In ancient Greek mythology Charon was the boatman who ferried the dead across the river Styx to the Underworld [Eds].

75. *high-flown, pedantic Greek.* Here the Shadow-show has a sly dig at the Purist School that wished to transform the spoken language into an imitation of Ancient Greek [TS].

79. Sior Nionios, Stavrakas. The first three drafts included the name Morphonios between these two. It was deleted by hand in the third draft and omitted altogether from the fourth. The omission is appropriate. In Act Two, although Morphonios turns up near the Dragon's den, he claims (page 71) that he has been instructed by the Pasha not to attempt to kill the dragon [Eds].

79. bow-string. The Sultan used to send a bow-string to any high official who fell under his displeasure. It was a hint that he should hang himself with it, or suffer a more painful death [TS].

80. yataghan. A short curved sword with no handguard [Eds].

82. inguinal. A medical term meaning "to do with the groin". Not present in the first three drafts but added by Stephanides in the final draft [Eds].

Milton Keynes UK
Ingram Content Group UK Ltd.
UKHW010042201123
432895UK00003B/14